Government and Politics of Northern Ireland

Third Edition

Dr Margery McMahon

Colourpoint
Educational

Third Edition
First Impression

© Margery McMahon
  1st edition 2002,
  2nd edition 2004
  3rd edition (much revised) 2008

Designed by Colourpoint Books
Printed by W&G Baird Ltd

ISBN 978 1 904242 95 6

About the author

Margery A McMahon graduated from Queens University Belfast with BA Hons in History and Politics. She continued her studies at the University of Glasgow and gained an MPhil (with distinction) and a PhD. Formerly a teacher of History and Politics, Margery now works in the Faculty of Education, University of Glasgow where she is a Senior Lecturer and Head of the Department of Educational Studies.

Colourpoint Books
Colourpoint House
Jubilee Business Park
21 Jubilee Road
Newtownards
County Down
Northern Ireland
BT23 4YH
Tel: 028 9182 6339
Fax: 028 9182 1900
E-mail: sales@colourpoint.co.uk
Web-site: www.colourpoint.co.uk

Contents

Acknowledgements

Many people have assisted me in producing this publication. In this 3rd edition I would like to pay particular acknowledgement and thanks to Sheila Johnston and Una McCann of Colourpoint publishers, to my former teaching colleagues at Loreto College, Coleraine, to my current colleagues at University of Glasgow and especially the many teachers that I have had the pleasure of working with in recent years through the Chartered Teacher initiative. A special word of thanks goes to Professor Christine Forde, Chair of Leadership and Professional Learning, University of Glasgow, from whom I have learned much.   *Margery McMahon July 2008*

Terminology

The term Good Friday Agreement (GFA) is used throughout this publication in reference to the political agreement reached on 10 April 1998. It is recognised, nevertheless, that this settlement is also referred to as the Belfast Agreement and that these terms are interchangeable. However, in order to avoid confusion when the abbreviated form is used – GFA as opposed to BA – it was decided to employ Good Friday Agreement as the descriptive term.

Abbreviations

AIA	Anglo Irish Agreement	NICRA	Northern Ireland Civil Rights Association
APNI	Alliance Party of Northern Ireland		
BIC	British Irish Council	NIHRC	Northern Ireland Human Rights Commission
CLMC	Combined Loyalist Military Command		
		NISRA	Northern Ireland Statistics and Research Agency
DFM	Deputy First Minister		
DSD	Department of Social Development	NSMC	North South Ministerial Council
DUP	Democratic Unionist Party	OUP	Official Unionist Party
EC	Executive committee	PM	Prime Minister
FM	First Minister	PR	Proportional Representation
FPTP	First Past the Post	PUP	Progressive Unionist Party
GB	Great Britain	PSNI	Police Service of Northern Ireland
GFA	Good Friday Agreement	RUC	Royal Ulster Constabulary
IRA	Irish Republican Army	RoI	Republic of Ireland
MLA	Member of the Legislative Assembly	SDLP	Social Democratic and Labour Party
MSP	Member of the Scottish Assembly	SF	Sinn Féin
MWA	Member of the Welsh Assembly	SOSNi	Secretary of State for Northern Ireland
NI	Northern Ireland	STV	Single Transferable Vote
NIO	Northern Ireland Office	UUC	Ulster Unionist Council
NILP	Northern Ireland Labour Party	UUP	Ulster Unionist Party

Introduction

THE ENDING OF THE 'Troubles' in Northern Ireland proved to be a protracted and complex process, characterised by negotiation and compromise, regression to violence, restoration of Direct Rule and intervention by British, Irish and American leaders endeavouring to secure a lasting peace. This process began in December 1993, with the signing of the Downing Street Declaration, though arguably, there had been less high profile efforts to bring an end to the conflict throughout the 1980s. The Downing Street Declaration set in train a process of negotiation and compromise which made possible the Good Friday Agreement of 1998 (also known as the Belfast Agreement), leading to the elections to the new Northern Ireland Assembly in May 1998, the setting up of the Northern Ireland Executive to govern the province and the establishment of 'devolved government' to Northern Ireland in 1999.

At the time, the Good Friday Agreement was hailed as 'historic' and indeed it was. However, it left a number of issues unresolved, most notably the status of paramilitary organisations and the issues of decommissioning of weapons and prisoner releases. Continued paramilitary activity and lack of resolution relating to decommissioning were ultimately to bring down the devolved administration that the Good Friday Agreement had achieved. This occurred not just once, but on four occasions (February 2000, August 2001, September 2001 and October 2002, NIO, 2008). After the latter dissolution, the NI Assembly went into a prolonged period of suspension lasting until May 2007.

The Assembly, established in May 2007 following the elections in March, was the result of a new agreement – The St Andrews Agreement – reached in Scotland in October 2006. While this agreement did not supersede or replace the Good Friday Agreement, it did attempt to close outstanding political loopholes and make possible the restoration of devolved government.

Much had changed in Northern Ireland in the intervening period between the signing of the Belfast Agreement and St Andrews Agreements and the ending of devolved government in 2002 and its restoration in 2007. A more buoyant economy, evident in property development and inward investment, suggested that the peace dividend was beginning to bear fruit. Reform of policing saw the former Royal Ulster Constabulary (RUC) complete the transition to becoming the Police Service of Northern Ireland (PSNI), recruiting more Catholics and women to serve in it and gaining support across NI's communities.

The political landscape had changed too. Many of Northern Ireland's politi
leaders, who had played a key role in the peace process and served in the first Assembl
were no longer directly involved, for example because of retirement, electoral def
or untimely death, such as David Irvine, leader of the Progressive Unionist Party,
January 2007. Electorally, gains for the Democratic Unionist Party (DUP) and Si
Féin (SF) saw them first displace and then replace the Ulster Unionist Party (UU
and Social Democratic Labour Party (SDLP) respectively as the traditional forces
constitutional unionism and nationalism.

The momentum of change in political life continued in 2008 with the resignati
of the First Minister, Ian Paisley, in June and his replacement by Peter Robinson. W
the resignation of Bertie Ahern as Taoiseach, in May 2008, many of the architects
the Good Friday Agreement and the St Andrews Agreement were no longer direc
involved in Northern Ireland Affairs (British PM, Tony Blair, had stepped down fro
office in June 2007; Ulster Unionist Leader, David Trimble, had stood down as pa
leader after the party's routing in the 2005 General Election; and John Hume a
Seamus Mallon of the SDLP had both retired). As the profile of the Assembly elected
2007 showed, the old guard was gradually giving way to the next generation.

Elsewhere in the United Kingdom the other devolved administrations in Scotland a
Wales continued to consolidate devolved government, becoming more confident a
assertive in their relations with the political centre at Westminster and in implementi
distinctive regional/national policies. With the enlargement of the European Union
2004, ten new states[1] joined the EU and the opening of borders led to a growing strea
of immigrants travelling to the UK in search of better opportunities. Many fou
their way to Northern Ireland, slowly changing the composition of a hitherto larg
homogeneous, albeit polarised society.[2]

In the first decade of the 21st century, Northern Ireland is a changed and changi
political entity, with the transition from conflict towards lasting peace almost compl
and devolved government restored once more. The focus of this book is governme
and politics in Northern Ireland under devolved government. To understand t
current arrangements for and operation of devolved government, it is necessary
review how these arrangements were agreed and developed. An appreciation of t
historical development of the Northern Ireland State is essential for this. A sh
overview of the history of the Northern Ireland State from its founding in 1921
the 1993 Downing Street Declaration, marking the beginning of the peace proce
is provided in Chapter 1. Pathways to peace, including the Belfast Agreement (199
and the St Andrews Agreement (2006), are explored in Chapter 2. The operatio
arrangements for the Northern Ireland Assembly and the Executive are outlined a
discussed in Chapter 3. Chapter 4 charts developments relating to the main Northe
Ireland political parties since 1994 and explores the consequences for them of devolv
government. This is linked to distinctive features of the Northern Irish Electoral Syst
which are examined in Chapter 5. A critical evaluation of key developments und
devolved government is provided in Chapter 6 and the conclusion, Chapter 7, offer

synopsis of government and politics in Northern Ireland while identifying the potential for consensus or contention in the future.

Notes

[1] These were Cyprus, Czech Republic, Estonia, Hungary, Latvia, Lithuania, Malta, Poland, Slovakia, Slovenia (BBC Online 2008)

[2] The last census for Northern was conducted in 2001 with the next one scheduled for 2011. Consequently this does not capture the increase in the number of migrant workers since 2004. The number of National Insurance Numbers (NINos) issued by the NIO gives some indication of the scale of this. For example in 2004-05, 5,826 were issued to non UK nationals. Of this, 752 were Poles. In 2005-06, the number of NINos issued increased to 15,614, of which 5,460 were issued to Polish nationals (DSD, 2007 – NISRA, 2008 – Table 1.12 NINo). According to the 2001 census, the population of Northern Ireland was 1,685,267 (NISRA online 2008)

Chapter 1
Government and Politics of
Northern Ireland in historical context

This chapter provides a short overview of the development of the Northern Ireland State from its founding in 1921 to the 1993 Downing Street Declaration, marking the beginning of the 'peace process'.

By the end of the chapter you will know:

- how and why the Northern Ireland state was set up;
- the circumstances leading to the introduction of Direct Rule in 1972;
- how Northern Ireland was governed under Direct Rule;
- the various attempts at seeking a resolution to the conflict, culminating in the Downing Street Declaration (1993).

SINCE ITS FOUNDATION, THE history of Northern Ireland has been characterised by two key trends: attempts by the British government to disengage from NI; and the breakdown of law and order leading to armed conflict which has effectively kept it involved since the restoration of direct rule in 1972. Since then there have been a number of attempts to broker a peace agreement, acceptable to all parties, which would enable self government to be returned to the people of Northern Ireland.

This gained impetus since 1993, with the signing of the Downing Street Declaration between the British and Irish governments, marking the beginning of a peace process which has lasted until 2008.

In this chapter, Northern Ireland's development from its foundation in 1921 is explored, providing an historical foundation for understanding the political developments of more recent years.

The establishment of Northern Ireland

The Northern Ireland state, as formally constituted in the Government of Ireland Act (1920), came into being in 1921. This small state (or statelet, as some prefer to call it) consisted of six of the nine counties of the historic province of Ulster. Generally these counties had a greater proportion of Protestants than Catholics living there.

Since the campaigns for Home Rule in the nineteenth century, unionists had mounted often violent and ultimately effective resistance to any proposal for Irish independence. The Government of Ireland Act, which conceded the right to govern themselves in their own state, was seen as a measure both of the extent to which the Ulster Unionists had threatened the British government and of the British government's gratitude for Northern Ireland's contribution to the British war effort in World War I. Nationalists and republicans in the new Irish Free State greatly resented the division of Ireland which the Dáil had acceded to in the Anglo-Irish Treaty (1921) and which was to be the cause of a bitter civil war in the years that followed.

In NI, democratic procedures and institutions were set up, but the effective disengagement of many of NI's Catholics and nationalists from the political process meant that parliament and government were largely dominated by unionists. Their sense of alienation was compounded by NI Prime Minister James Craig's response in 1934 to de Valera's (the Irish Taoiseach) remark about the place of Catholicism in Ireland, that "we are a Protestant Parliament and a Protestant State" (Buckland, 1981:55). In terms of demographic distribution, Protestants dominated in the six counties that made up NI. The Catholic population was in the minority, though in some counties it constituted a substantial minority and in some towns, such as Derry, they formed the majority. Once the new structures were in place, formally recognised by the visit of the King and Queen for the state opening of Parliament in 1921, the British government essentially disengaged from direct involvement in NI affairs.

Parliament and government in NI, 1921–1972

In terms of constitutional structures, Northern Ireland was based on the Westminster model, ie a bicameral system, though unlike Westminster, the lower house, the Commons, elected the members of the upper house, the Senate.

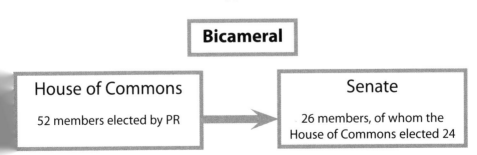

Bicameral

House of Commons

52 members elected by PR

Senate

26 members, of whom the House of Commons elected 24

In selecting proportional representation (PR) as the preferred electoral system for the new NI legislature, it appeared that a commitment to democracy and democratic procedures would be one of the core foundations of the new state. Though relatively untried, many of the new states, which emerged in Europe after World War I, embraced PR as a way of underpinning democracy, which Germany's aggression had threatened to undermine. The experiment with PR in NI was to be relatively short-lived. PR was abolished first in local elections in 1922 and subsequently in parliamentary elections in 1929. The result of the former was to reduce nationalist representation at local level, but the latter mainly affected the Northern Ireland Labour Party (NILP) and Unionist independents.

The Northern Ireland government was headed by a prime minister and a cabinet of ministers from the party which had won a majority in the election.

The powers devolved to NI's government in the Government of Ireland Act (1920) were limited and ultimately could be rescinded. Section 75 of the Act left sovereignty of NI with the British Parliament. Westminster retained responsibility for matters of the Crown, defence, external trade and international relations in addition to taxation, postal services and the Supreme Court of NI. In domestic affairs the remit of the NI government was wide, having responsibility for education, health, personal and social services, law and order, housing, planning and economic development.

Nationalists in Northern Ireland

The response of NI's nationalist minority to the newly devolved government and parliament was to disassociate itself from it. In the first elections to the new House of Commons, Unionists were victorious. The new Parliament, elected on 24 May 1921, was made up of 40 Unionists, 6 Nationalists and 6 Sinn Féin representatives. When the first session of the Parliament met, the Nationalist and Sinn Féin representatives did not attend. This meant that the members of the Senate, elected by the members of the Commons, were all Protestant.

Effectively, Catholics and nationalists in NI were not adequately represented at parliamentary level. While it could be argued that this was the result of their disengagement from the state and its institutions, to which they were opposed, it can also be said that the state did little to encourage their active involvement and indeed often militated against it. In the early years of the new state, republicans showed their opposition to and alienation from it by violent protest, further polarising the community between unionist and nationalist, Protestant and Catholic.

In later years the Nationalist Party represented nationalists in Parliament, but as a minority party in a unionist-dominated Parliament they were rarely able to exert much influence. Consequently the NI government, backed by a loyal Parliament, could govern unchallenged and unregulated by either an effective parliamentary opposition or by the British government.

The preferential position enjoyed by unionists in political, but also in economic terms meant that nationalists, as the minority, perceived themselves to be openly discriminated against. This was most marked in areas such as housing and employment but was also evident in education and social and health provision. Growing resentment at this discrimination led many to support the Civil Rights movement, which emerged in 1967.

The emergence of the Civil Rights movement in NI resulted in the mobilisation of large numbers of NI's Catholics, and many of its Protestants, against perceived injustices. Under the pressure of popular protest, the reforming Ulster Unionist PM, Terence O'Neill, acceded to many of the demands of the movement. The Civil Rights movement, and the response of the NI government to it, brought to the surface existing intercommunal divisions which had until recently been suppressed. Many Protestants equated civil rights with Catholic rights, and believed that they were now becoming the victims of discrimination. Within the 'Official' Unionist Party (OUP) and O'Neill's government there were many who believed that the PM had gone too far. At the local level, relations between Protestant and Catholic communities deteriorated: as the Civil Rights marches went through Protestant areas, the marchers were attacked and the police appeared to do little to stop it. Increasingly, Catholics and nationalists became less confident about the ability of the government and the police to protect them from sectarian attacks; into this perceived gap came a reformed and rearmed Irish Republican Army (IRA). Meanwhile, the British government, similarly doubtful about the ability of the NI government and police force to manage a worsening situation, deployed the British army in NI. By 1969 Northern Ireland had descended into the sectarian conflict that was to last for almost 30 years.

The Civil Rights movement effectively ended in January 1972 when thirteen demonstrators at a Civil Rights march in Derry were shot dead by British soldiers. By the summer of 1972 the British government was no longer convinced of the ability of the NI government and its new PM, Brian Faulkner, to deal with the situation and felt that they were exacerbating it. When the British PM, Edward Heath, refused Faulkner's requests for the rearming of the Royal Ulster Constabulary (RUC), Faulkner and the government resigned and the British government prorogued the NI Parliament. For the first time in 51 years, Northern Ireland was to be governed directly from Westminster.

Direct rule

Direct rule was intended to be a temporary solution to the problem of governing NI. That it took so long to reach an agreement acceptable to all those involved is evidence of the complexity and intricacies of Northern Ireland politics.

During the period of direct rule Northern Ireland was administered by Westminster through a Secretary of State for Northern Ireland (SoSNI). This was a government minister responsible for NI affairs, appointed by the PM. The SoSNI was supported in this role by a number of junior ministers. As prime ministerial appointees, the Secretary of State and the junior ministers were usually British MPs who often knew little about Northern Ireland and its people. This detachment from and lack of familiarity with Northern Ireland affairs represented the 'democratic deficit', which existed in Northern Ireland during direct rule. The Northern Ireland electorate now had no control over those who were governing them. NI sent 12 MPs to Westminster where their influence was felt only when a government majority was under threat. (The number of MPs from NI was increased to 17 at the 1983 general election and to 18 at the 1997 election.)

Few anticipated that direct rule would last so long and throughout the period efforts were made by the British government, NI's politicians and the government of the Republic of Ireland to reach a solution and end the violence. Soon after the proroguing of the NI Parliament in 1972, the British government began initiatives to restore self-government to NI. However, the resulting power-sharing Executive of 1973–4 was to be short-lived, brought down amidst Protestant opposition in the form of the Ulster Workers' Council strike of 1974. Unionist opposition had hardened after the Sunningdale Agreement of 1973 (between the British and Irish governments and the NI Executive), which had proposed a Council of Ireland. Further attempts to work towards achieving a political solution to Northern Ireland's problems foundered against the backdrop of ongoing sectarian violence. An attempt in 1982 to restore self-government to NI through a process of 'rolling devolution' failed due to the absence of cross-party support. Following the elections for a new Assembly, only the Unionist and Alliance Party (APNI) representatives took their seats, with the nationalist Social

Democratic and Labour Party (SDLP) maintaining an abstentionist position. In the absence of participants representing all parties in NI, the Assembly could achieve little and was dissolved in 1986.

Democratic Deficit

This is a term used to describe occasions when voters are unable to experience the full benefits of political representation due to shortcomings in the electoral system or political structure. In the Northern Ireland context the period of direct rule is seen as contributing to the 'democratic deficit' as the people of Northern Ireland had little say over the people who governed and had limited ability to influence decisions affecting them. It is also seen as "the profusion of unelected quangos which passed for local participation in government during the long years of direct rule" (BBC NI On-line 3 May 2003).

The term 'democratic deficit' is used in a range of political perspectives, though it is often used in relation to the European Union. In this context 'democratic deficit' is defined as "a concept invoked principally in the argument that the European Union and its various bodies suffer from a lack of democracy and seem inaccessible to the ordinary citizen because their method of operating is so complex" (Europa Glossary On-line 2008). In the UK context the term is increasingly used to describe the perceived inequity of devolved powers ceded to Scotland, Wales and Northern Ireland and the absence of such powers for England.

The persistence of 'a democratic deficit' in NI in recent years is discussed in Chapter 3.

At intergovernmental level some progress was made, culminating in the signing of the Anglo-Irish Agreement (AIA) in 1985. In retrospect, the AIA can be viewed as an important turning point in Anglo-Irish relations. The RoI retained its constitutional claim to the six counties of NI and unionists were assured of a veto against unification as long as they were a majority in NI. Both sides committed themselves to working to achieve lasting peace and stability by peaceful means and through agreement, stressing co-operation and the joint fight against terrorism. The new relationship was to form the basis of intergovernmental co-operation in the following years, though it was often tested to the limits by ongoing unionist opposition to the AIA and continued violence. Unionists opposed the AIA because it gave the RoI a recognised role in NI affairs. Many unionists feared that the AIA would mark the beginning of a process of gradual reunification of both parts of Ireland.

In the late 1980s and early 1990s, despite ongoing violence which resulted in many deaths and casualties and the destruction of homes and businesses, talks to try to seek a solution to NI's problems took place at various levels, including intergovernmental and interparty.

A new Secretary of State for NI, Peter Brooke, was appointed in July 1989. A few months later, in November, he issued a statement that the Provisional IRA (PIRA) could not be defeated militarily and that if, and when, IRA violence ended he would not rule out speaking to SF. In January 1991, in a bid to restart the political process, Brooke launched talks between NI's constitutional parties. The talks were short-lived – on February 9, 1991 the IRA bombed Downing Street. This seemed to confirm Brooke's earlier statement – now the IRA had succeeded in striking at the heart of British power. The SoSNI tried to re-ignite the talks process again in early July 1991, but these talks broke up without having advanced beyond procedural issues.

The general election of April 1992 saw the Conservatives returned to power under John Major with a slim majority. This position greatly increased the bargaining power of the Unionist MPs at Westminster. In NI, SF's rise appeared to have been thwarted by the loss of Gerry Adam's Westminster seat to Joe Hendron of the SDLP. The elections also saw a drop in the DUP's share of the vote. The time seemed apt for a new round of talks to be initiated. Hence, a new SoSNI, Sir Patrick Mayhew, began a fresh talks process in April 1992, with progress made on issues such as the structure of the NI legislature and executive.

The publication of SF's document *Towards a lasting peace in Ireland* in 1992 had prompted the SDLP leader, John Hume, to pursue secret talks with SF's leader, Gerry Adams. Hume was partly motivated by a wish to avoid failure, especially in view of the collapse of the official talks, and by a belief in the need to find a way to involve SF in any talks that would ensure a lasting peace. Thus began a series of talks and negotiations between the SDLP and SF leaders, which were in large part responsible for the inclusion of SF in all-party talks once their ceasefire was in place.

In April 1993 Hume and Adams issued a joint statement declaring that an internal settlement of the NI political situation without "an Irish dimension" was not a solution. They said that the Irish people as a whole have "a right to national self-determination" and acknowledged that the consent and allegiance of unionists were essential ingredients if "a lasting peace was to be established". Unionists reacted angrily to the revelation of talks, issuing declarations condemning the 'pan-nationalist front'.

While Hume and Adams were talking secretly, the Irish and British governments continued with intergovernmental talks which resulted in the Downing Street Declaration of December 1993. The British government's admission that it had "no selfish strategic or economic interest in Northern Ireland" was taken as a sign of its commitment to reach a settlement. The declaration stated that its primary interest was to see "peace, stability and reconciliation established by agreement among all people who inhabit the island". The role of the British government, it foresaw, was to "encourage, facilitate and enable" the achievement of such agreement over time, through a process of dialogue and co-operation, based on full respect for the rights and identities of both traditions in Ireland. The Declaration acknowledged that this might take the form of a united Ireland, which would be decided by the people of Ireland on ie basis of consent, through concurrent referenda.

The Downing Street Declaration laid the foundation for intergovernmental co-operation in subsequent years, and though it did not bring an immediate end to the violence in Northern Ireland, the agreement of the two governments to cooperate in finding a way to end the conflict was an important milestone in Northern Ireland's transition away from conflict and towards lasting peace.

Summary

The Northern Ireland state was set up as a consequence of the compromise reached by the British government with the new government of the Irish Free State in 1921, in which Ireland was partitioned and the demands of the Unionist majority in Northern Ireland to remain part of the United Kingdom were acceded to.

From 1921–1972 Northern Ireland was governed by its own politicians but tensions between the Unionist-dominated government and state and the sizeable Catholic and largely nationalist minority existed and escalated in the 1960s with the emergence of the Civil Rights movement. Tensions between the two communities in Northern Ireland heightened and soon led to armed conflict, forcing the British government to intervene for the first time since the 1920s, by sending the British army to support NI's police force in containing the conflict. As the conflict grew, the NI government proved incapable of resolving it, leading the British government to prorogue the NI government and govern NI directly from Westminster. During this period of direct rule, government of NI was in the hands of a Secretary of State, appointed by the Prime Minister and supported by a team of ministers. These were not locally elected politicians representing the interests of the NI electorate and this is seen as resulting in a 'democratic deficit'. There were various attempts at seeking a resolution to the conflict such as the Sunningdale Agreement (1973) and the Anglo Irish Agreement (1985) but it was the Downing Street Declaration in 1993 that was to lay the foundation stone for the 'peace process' that developed in the 1990s.

Chapter 2
Pathways to Peace

In this chapter the key milestones of the Northern Ireland 'peace process' are explored and evaluated. These include the Good Friday Agreement (1998) and the St Andrews Agreement (2006) – two key agreements in shaping the structure of Northern Ireland's devolved executive and legislature.

By the end of the chapter you will know:

- how agreement was reached on the nature of devolved government in Northern Ireland;

- the key features of the agreements and their implications for devolved government.

FEW ANTICIPATED THAT REACHING a resolution of the Northern Ireland conflic would take so long and that the 'peace process' would be so prolonged. Conflic resolution elsewhere has shown that an agreement to end conflict does not brin immediate peace and stability. In this respect, the pathway to peace in Northern Irelan was very much a 'process' – of bargaining, negotiation, compromise, concessior *testing each other* brinkmanship and agreement. The guarding of traditional political beliefs and the nee to assuage the fears of respective communities has meant small, confidence-buildin and trust-making steps have had to follow the big leaps at party political level an within and between communities.

Consistent throughout this process has been the commitment of the British an Irish governments to bring an end to the conflict and to seek an intergovernmenta agreement that would restore parliamentary democracy and self government t Northern Ireland in an agreed form of power-sharing.

 *ie; Israel & Palestine*

How was agreement reached on the nature of devolved government in Northern Ireland?

The first stage in this process was the joint declaration made by the British and Irish governments in December 1993. Having admitted that it had "no selfish strategic or economic interest in Northern Ireland" the British government stated that its primary interest was to see "peace, stability and reconciliation established by agreement among all people who inhabit the island". Its role would be to "encourage, facilitate and enable" the achievement of such agreement over time, through a process of dialogue and co-operation, based on full respect for the rights and identities of both traditions in Ireland. In the Declaration, the British government acknowledged that this might take the form of a united Ireland, decided by the people of Ireland through concurrent referenda (Downing Street Declaration, 1993).

Albert Reynolds, the Irish Taoiseach, responded by saying that in the event of an overall political settlement, the Irish government would put forward and support proposals for changing the Irish constitution which would fully represent the principle of consent in NI (*ibid*). Both governments stated that democratically mandated parties which were committed to exclusively peaceful methods and democratic processes could participate in the talks.

What was significant about this Declaration was that hitherto historic positions were being set aside and with these perceived 'obstacles' removed, a path might be created which would allow NI's political parties to negotiate an end to the conflict. In the case of the British government, the renouncing of any selfish and strategic interest in NI was designed to provide assurances to the republican and nationalist community. Meanwhile the RoI's offer to revise its constitution sought to reassure Unionists and Loyalists of its intent to preserve the border unless or until determined otherwise in a democratic way.

The Downing Street Declaration paved the wave for the IRA ceasefire in August 1994, with the announcement that there would be "complete cessation of military operations". With the ceasefire in place, the decommissioning of weapons became a serious issue. The fact that the IRA had not spoken about a "permanent ceasefire" led to calls for decommissioning to be made a precondition of entry into any future talks. A loyalist ceasefire did not occur until October 1994, when an announcement to that effect was made by the Combined Loyalist Military Command (CLMC).

The impetus for multi-party talks driven by the British and Irish governments continued in subsequent months with the publication in February 1995 of the Framework Document containing proposals for a one-chamber assembly of 90 members elected by PR and chaired by a directly elected panel of three people. Unionists rejected the Framework Document, claiming that there was little to distinguish it from the Sunningdale Agreement (1973) and the Council of Ireland.

Nevertheless, the drive towards a settlement continued, with the aim to achieve agreement on the basis of future all-party talks by the end of February 1996. Parties

17

were invited to preparatory talks. As part of this twin track approach, an international body, led by US Senator George Mitchell, was tasked with looking into the question of decommissioning. He reported that the paramilitary organisations would not decommission arms before all-party talks but proposed a compromise that:

"... to reach an agreed political settlement and to take the gun out of Irish politics, there must be commitment and adherence to fundamental principles of democracy and non-violence. Participants in all-party negotiations should affirm their commitment to such principles". (Mitchell Report, 1996)

Senator Mitchell's Report concluded: "The risk may seem high but the reward is great: a future of peace, equality and prosperity for all the people of Northern Ireland." (Mitchell Report, 1996).

Multi-party talks were seriously jeopardised by the ending of the IRA ceasefire in February 1996, when an IRA bomb exploded in the centre of Canary Wharf, London. The end of the ceasefire meant that Sinn Féin would be excluded from any peace talks, and Canary Wharf had underlined for both governments the importance of continued efforts to reach a settlement. A Northern Ireland Forum was proposed which would be made up of elected representatives and which would initiate all-party talks, beginning in June 1996. Participants had to agree to the Mitchell Principles before being permitted to participate. From the parties participating in the NI Forum, nominations would be made for delegates for negotiations with the British and Irish governments. These negotiations were to be chaired by Senator Mitchell.

All-party talks began in June 1996, but were given a fresh impetus with the election of a new Labour government in Britain in May 1997. At the general election, Sinn Féin received an electoral endorsement for it policies, evident in its share of the vote rising from 10% (1992 general election) to 16%. In July 1997 the IRA ceasefire was resumed and Sinn Féin entered the talks in September. The deadline for a settlement was finalised as May 1998, and the SoSNI, Mo Mowlam, timetabled a referendum in NI and, with the agreement of the Taoiseach, a concurrent referendum in the RoI. Protracted negotiations over many months, and working through the night in the final hours, produced the Good Friday Agreement (Belfast Agreement) of May 1998.

The Good Friday Agreement (1998)

The Good Friday Agreement (GFA) marked an important juncture in Northern Ireland's history. That agreement was finally reached under pressure of a looming deadline and the glare of international media, who were camped in the grounds of Stormont, all the while adding to the drama of the outcome. The British Prime Minister, Tony Blair, captured the historic nature of the moment when he said how he felt "the hand of history" shortly before the agreement was signed (*Guardian Unlimited*, 2008).

However, even in 1998 the unravelling of the agreement was predicted by many, though even the most hardened nay-sayers could not have forecast the lengthy and protracted effort required to sustain devolved government, and to restore it after suspension, especially following the proroguing of the Assembly in 2002. Nevertheless, the Good Friday Agreement provided an agreed structure for government in Northern Ireland, and while aspects of the agreement required amendment in the St Andrews Agreement in 2006, this did not constitute a renegotiation or rewriting of the original agreement, and it continues to provide the basis for the devolved administration in NI that was restored in May 2007.

Any political agreement acceptable to all of NI's political parties needed to provide mechanisms to:

- determine an acceptable form of power-sharing in which both communities would be fairly and proportionally represented;
- retain and legitimise the link with GB;
- define an acceptable role for the RoI.

An acceptable form of power-sharing was achieved in the GFA through the election of MLAs using the single transferable vote (STV) form of PR. Ministerial positions in the Executive Committee (EC) would be allocated in proportion to the electoral strength of the political parties. This represented an important shift in unionist thinking away from the idea of majority rule towards an acceptance of the principles of consociationalism (see page 30 for an explanation of this term). Unionist fears about the prospect of a united Ireland were allayed with the embedding in the GFA of the principle of consent and the commitment of the RoI to revoke Articles 2 and 3 of its constitution.

Retaining and legitimising the link with GB was achieved in the GFA through the creation of the British-Irish Council (BIC), or the Council of the Isles. This development assuaged unionist fears that with a power-sharing Assembly the link with GB would be severed, leading inevitably to a united Ireland (a brief outline of the BIC is provided in Chapter 6).

The role of the RoI had proved an area of contention in previous negotiations and talks regarding a settlement. For nationalists a settlement would not be acceptable unless there was recognition of the link with RoI and a formalisation of that link. Unionists, however, objected to any role for the RoI which included executive powers or the potential to acquire these powers. The compromise was reached through the North/South Ministerial Council (NSMC) (a brief outline of the NSMC is provided in Chapter 6).

In the final published agreement all these issues were dealt with under distinct strands. The table on page 20 illustrates this.

Popular endorsement for the Agreement was given in referenda held in Northern Ireland and in the Republic of Ireland on 22 May 1998. Respondents in NI were asked: "Do you support the Agreement reached at the multi-party talks on Northern Ireland?" Turnout for the referendum in NI was 81.1% of which 71.1% voted Yes and 28.9% voted No. In RoI, voters were asked to give approval to amending the Constitution in relation to Articles 2 and 3, when the GFA came into force.[1] Turnout here was not *[to page 21]*

The Good Friday Agreement (10 April 1998)

GFA Strand	Focus	Extract from Agreement
Strand 1	Democratic Institutions in Northern Ireland	This agreement provides for a democratically elected Assembly in Northern Ireland which is <u>inclusive</u> in its membership, capable of exercising executive and legislative authority, and subject to safeguards to protect the rights and interests of all sides of the community. *Strand 1, Article 1, The Good Friday Agreement, 1998 (p5)*
Strand 2	North South Ministerial Council	Under a new British/Irish Agreement dealing with the totality of relationships, and related legislation at Westminster and in the Oireachtas, a North/South Ministerial Council is to be established to bring together those with executive responsibilities in Northern Ireland and the Irish Government, to develop consultation, cooperation and action within the island of Ireland – including through implementation on an all-island and cross border basis – on matters of mutual interest within the competence of the Administrations, North and South. *Strand 2, Article 1, The Good Friday Agreement, 1998 (p11)*
Strand 3	British Irish Council	A British-Irish Council (BIC) will be established under a new British Irish Agreement to promote the harmonious and mutually beneficial development of the totality of relationships among the peoples of these islands. *Strand 3, Article 1, The Good Friday Agreement, 1998 (p14)*
Additional issues	• Rights, Safeguards and Equality of Opportunity • Decommissioning • Security • Policing and Justice • Prisoners	*GFA* p19 *GFA* p20 *GFA* p21 *GFA* p22 *GFA* p25

as high as in NI (55.6 %) but most of those who voted were overwhelmingly in favour, 94.4% with only 5.6% voting No.

Table 1 *Results and turnout for concurrent referenda on the Good Friday Agreement*

	Northern Ireland	Republic of Ireland
% Yes	✳ 71.1%	94.4%
% No	28.9%	5.6%
Turnout – ppl	81.1%	55.6%

Know figures.

who were eligible to vote.

With popular support for the GFA in both North and South assured, the path was clear for the next stage in the schedule for devolved government: elections to the Northern Ireland Assembly. (The electoral arrangements and structures for elections in Northern Ireland are fully outlined in Chapter 5.)

Elections for the new multi-party Assembly were held on 25 June 1998. The table below shows the results of the first elections to the new Northern Ireland Assembly.

Table 2 *Party share of Assembly Seats after 1998 Assembly Election*

Political Party	Number of Assembly Seats
Ulster Unionist Party	28
Social Democratic and Labour Party	24
Democratic Unionist Party	20
Sinn Féin	18
Alliance Party	6
United Kingdom Unionist Party	5
Progressive Unionist Party	2
Northern Ireland Women's Coalition	2
Others	3
Total	**108**

Northern Ireland's elected representative, known as MLAs (Members of the Legislative Assembly) were elected using the Single Transferable Vote (STV) voting system, which is a form of proportional representation (PR). This type of electoral system aims to combine constituency representation with proportionality. There are multi-member constituencies in which voters state their electoral preference numerically by placing 1, 2, and 3 and so on against the names of their preferred candidates. Once the election has taken place, all the votes in a constituency are counted and a quota is established which a candidate must attain in order to be elected. When the candidate has attained the quota, the second preference votes of the voters are redistributed to the other selected candidates. This system benefits smaller parties, which can get parliamentary seats through second- and third- preference votes.

In the 1998 election to the new Assembly, 108 MLAs were elected from the existing 18 Westminster constituencies in Northern Ireland, with six representatives elected from each constituency. As Table 2 shows, the parties with the largest number of seats in the Assembly were the UUP and SDLP, and so leaders from these two parties formed the Executive, with David Trimble from the UUP becoming First Minister, and Seamus Mallon, from the SDLP, Deputy First Minister. Seats on the NI Executive were allocated on the basis of a party's share of the vote, using a system of electoral allocation known as D'Hondt. The positions of Chair and Deputy Chair of the Assembly Committees were also allocated using this system.

In 1998, STV benefited smaller parties such as the Progressive Unionist Party (PUP) and the Northern Ireland Women's Coalition (NIWC) which gained Assembly seats through second and third preference votes so although the larger parties predominated, smaller parties were able to make a contribution.

In the months following the elections, the Assembly met in shadow form[2] to prepare for full transfer of devolved powers. This occurred on 30 November 1999 when the Secretary of State introduced the Northern Ireland Act 1998 (Commencement Order No 5), resulting in the devolution of powers to the Northern Ireland Assembly from 2 December 1999 (Northern Ireland Assembly, 2008)

The first meeting of the NI Assembly and Executive under the devolved arrangements marked another important point in NI's development. In the months that followed, all elements of the GFA became operational including the North South Ministerial Council (NSMC – Strand 2, GFA) and the British-Irish Council (BIC – Strand 3, GFA).

However, the flawed nature of some aspects of the Agreement and outstanding, unresolved issues in the wider political context in NI – such as ongoing paramilitary activity – contributed to the difficulties experienced by the Assembly and NI Executive. These difficulties were manifest in periods of devolved government, interspersed by the restoration of direct rule from 1999–2007. The NI Assembly was suspended on four occasions: February 2000, August 2001, September 2001 and October 2002 (NIO, 2002). After its suspension in 2002, it was to be five years before devolved government was restored. In the intervening period, the British and Irish governments continued to seek a solution that would enable devolved government to be returned to Northern Ireland once more.

The political landscape in Northern Ireland had changed greatly in the period of suspension of the Assembly in 2002 and its restoration in 2007. Sinn Féin's electoral ascendancy continued, displacing the SDLP as the main party representing nationalists, while the UUP was eclipsed by the DUP – with the latter taking an increasingly hardened stance on the GFA. In the 2003 elections to the Assembly, which took place, even though the Assembly was in suspension, the polarisation between parties and within parties became more evident, with the smaller parties, which had gained in the first Assembly elections in 1998, squeezed.

Table 3 below shows the results of the 2003 elections to the NI Assembly.

Table 3 *Party share of Assembly Seats after 1998 and 2003 Assembly elections*

Political Party	Number of Assembly Seats	
	1998	2003
Ulster Unionist Party	28	27
Social Democratic and Labour Party	24	18
Democratic Unionist Party	20	30
Sinn Féin	18	24
Alliance Party	6	6
United Kingdom Unionist Party	5	1
Progressive Unionist Party	2	1
Northern Ireland Women's Coalition	2	0
Others	3	1
Total	108	108

The polarisation continued during the prolonged period of suspension from 2002–2007, and it was clear in the 2007 Assembly elections, that the DUP and Sinn Féin had become dominant political forces in NI. The results of all three elections to the NI Assembly are provided in **Table 4**.

During the period of extended suspension, the British and Irish governments continued their efforts to reach agreement with and between NI's political parties to restore devolved government. A 'Comprehensive Agreement' in 2004 attempted to break the stalemate by providing a review of the GFA. The Agreement proposed institutional and procedural reforms to all three pillars of the political architecture crafted in 1998: the Assembly and the Executive, the North-South bodies and the British-Irish Council (Wilford & Wilson, April 2005:4). A key stumbling block was

Table 4 *Party share of Assembly Seats after 1998, 2003 and 2007 Assembly elections*

Political Party	1998	2003	2007
Ulster Unionist Party	28	27	18
Social Democratic and Labour Party	24	18	16
Democratic Unionist Party	20	30	36
Sinn Féin	18	24	28
Alliance Party	6	6	7
United Kingdom Unionist Party	5	1	
Progressive Unionist Party	2	1	
Northern Ireland Women's Coalition	2	0	
Others	3	1	3
Total	**108**	**108**	**108**

decommissioning and the demand from Unionist leaders for greater transparency on decommissioning, using photographic evidence (*ibid*). In the event, consensus could not be reached and the anticipated 'deal of deals' floundered.

Despite the collapse of the 'Comprehensive Agreement' both governments remained firm in their resolve to achieve agreement on restoring devolved government. They conveyed the seriousness of their endeavours in veiled threats about "enhanced partnership" between London and Dublin in the event of non compliance and resumption of direct rule, and the warning from the Secretary of State, Peter Hain, to the Assembly's Preparation for Government Committee that "devolution might not otherwise be restored for ten years" (Wilford and Wilson, January 2007:21). Events immediately subsequent to the collapse of the 'Comprehensive Agreement', (particularly the Northern Bank Raid in December 2004 and the murder of Belfast man Robert McCartney in January 2005) stretched even the most tolerant of political stakeholders, as well as many of NI's electorate, and brought firmly into the spotlight issues of alleged IRA criminality and matters of policing and law and order.

Pressure on the parties to reach an accommodation came with the setting of a final deadline for devolution for 24 November 2006. Negotiations took place at St Andrews in Scotland in October 2006, and agreement on a way forward was reached after concessions to both the DUP and SF. While some of the concessions became evident in the subsequent amendments to the GFA, other aspects began to emerge in the months after the summit and after the Assembly had reconvened.[3]

Unlike the GFA, the St Andrews Agreement was not so much an agreement among the parties as more an agreement on an agenda for moving forward (Wilford and Wilson, January 2007:22). A series of milestones set for the move to devolved government soon became flexible and the final deadline of 24 November became a deadline only for the nomination of first and deputy first ministers. NI's political parties were required to assent by 10 November 2007, though neither SF nor DUP did so by that date (*ibid*).

St Andrews Agreement 2006
Northern Ireland (St Andrews Agreement) Bill
Summary of Key features[4]

Part 1	**Transitional Assembly (1)**
Preparations for the restoration of devolved government	Establishment of Transitional Assembly by 24 November 2006; the May 2006 Assembly to cease to exist.
• Preparations for restoration of devolved government	The purpose of Transitional Assembly would be to make preparations for restoration of devolved government. (1:1a)
• Compliance or non-compliance with St Andrews Agreement timetable	The transitional assembly would embark on a programme of work designed to agree new standing orders for a new assembly, to draft a ministerial code and to prepare the ground for the Executive. (1:1b)
	Dissolution of the Transitional Assembly on 30 January 2007.
	Elections for new Assembly scheduled for 7 March 2007.
• Next Northern Ireland Assembly Election – March 2007	Deadline for devolution and formation of the Executive Committee – 26 March 2007.
• Remuneration of members of the Assembly	

Part 2	**Ministerial Conduct**
Amendments to the Northern Ireland Act 1998 etc	All Ministers or Junior Ministers to act in accordance with the provisions of the Ministerial Code (28A:I).
• Ministerial conduct	Ministerial decisions can be deferred to the Executive Committee if petitioned by 30 members of the Assembly, if a ministerial decision may have been taken in contravention of the Ministerial Code or if it relates to a matter of public importance (28 B:1)
• Ministerial appointment	The Ministerial Pledge of Office to include a commitment to: promote the interest of the whole community; to participate fully in the Executive Committee, NSMC and BIC; to uphold the rule of law; and endorsing and supporting of the PSNI and criminal justice system and institutions including the Policing Board.
• Committees	**Ministerial appointment**
• NSMC and BIC	The First Minister and Deputy First Ministers will be nominated by the Nominating officers of the largest political party of the first largest political designation and second largest political designation respectively (8:4&5). The persons nominated under subsections (4) and (5) shall not take up office until each of them has affirmed the terms of the pledge of office.
	Committees
	Standing orders will make provision for establishing a committee to examine such matters relating to the functioning of the Assembly and the Executive Committee as may be specified in the Standing orders (11:1).
	NSMC & BIC
	The First Minister and the Deputy First Minister acting jointly shall as far in advance of each meeting of the North South Ministerial Council or the British Irish council as is reasonably practicable, give to the Executive Committee and to the Assembly the following information in relation to the meetings: the date; the agenda; and the names of the Ministers and junior Ministers who are to attend the meeting (12:1).
	Each minister or junior Minister who has responsibility in relation to any matter included in the agenda for a meeting of either council shall be entitled to attend the meeting and to participate in the meeting so far as it relates to that matter (12:2).
	It shall be a Ministerial responsibility of each appropriate Minister or if a Minister or junior minister is nominated to attend a meeting of the NSMC or BIC to participate in the meeting so far as it relates to matters for which the appropriate Minister has responsibility (52B:1).

Part 3 Other amendments	
• District Policing Partnerships	Reconstitution of District Policing partnerships (Schedule 8) and District Policing Partnerships: Belfast Subgroups (Schedule 9)
• Education	Amendment of Education (NI) Order 2006
Part 4 Supplemental	Matters relating to implementation

It was widely accepted, even at the time of signing, that aspects of the GFA would require development, to close some of its political loopholes and to remove dubiety, both in interpretation and implementation. For example, Ministerial Responsibility, specified in the St Andrews Agreement, meant that Ministers could not refuse to take part in the meetings of the NSMC in the way that the DUP had refused to participate in the previous Executive. The provision in the 2006 Agreement for deferring Ministerial decisions to the Executive if petitioned by 30 MLAs sought to prevent the unilateral ministerial decision-making of the last devolved administration, such as the decision of the Minister for Education on the eve of the Assembly's suspension, to abolish the Eleven Plus examination. Perhaps of greatest significant was the amendment to the Ministerial Code, which required Ministers to endorse and support the PSNI and criminal justice system and institutions including the Policing Board, marking a significant step forward for Sinn Féin, which had previously refused recognition of these.

In this sense, the St Andrews Agreement did not mark the failure of the Good Friday Agreement, but rather another stage in its development, necessary to reflect the altered political context in NI that had emerged after 1998 and to take NI to the next stage.

The St Andrews Agreement required the assent of all political parties and for the DUP and SF – with strong caucuses within their own parties – progress was cautious, characterised by the political brinkmanship that has become a feature of political bargaining in the NI peace process. In SF's case, it was necessary to gain agreement from SF's Executive (*Ard Chomhairle*) to hold a party conference (*Ard Fheis*) on the question of policing. The Ard Fheis was held on 28 January 2007, and 900 party members voted to give support to the SF Executive motion to express its "critical support for civic policing through a police service which is representative of the community it serves, free from partisan political control and democratically accountable"; in essence, accepting the requirements of the St Andrews Agreement relating to policing and criminal justice (bbc.co.uk: 28/01/07, Wilford & Wilson: April 2007:12).

27

This cleared the way for the restoration of devolved government, following the Assembly Elections in March 2007. After almost five years Northern Ireland would be governed by its own democratically elected administration.

Summary

The path towards peace in NI was far from easy, characterised by many false dawns and political brinkmanship. Why then was it possible to reach a resolution in 2007, when it had proved so intractable previously? One view is that the key players saw it as a last chance to claim their historical legacy. Tony Blair, the British Prime Minister who had been instrumental in securing the GFA in 1998, was about to demit office as PM. In the latter years his tenure had been overshadowed by the war in Iraq. A last push at a deal in NI would deflect from this. For Ian Paisley, once the arch-opponent to sharing power with Sinn Féin, this was his chance to lead the state he had so vigorously defended over the years. And for Sinn Féin, assenting to the St Andrews Agreement finally brought them in from the political cold. However, the extent to which Northern Ireland had changed since the first days of the peace process should not be underestimated. The fragile peace that developed in NI, especially in the years after the GFA in 1998, enabled its citizens not only to experience the benefits of representative government but also to gain from the 'peace dividend' which brought investment and employment. Finally, the international context in which the paramilitary organisations had operated had changed and where once the terrorist threat was seen to be the IRA, in the years after 9/11, the perceived threat of Islamist terrorism provided a reflective lens for looking afresh at the NI problem and its resolution.

Notes

[1] Voters were asked 'Do you approve of the proposal to amend the Constitution contained in the under mentioned Bill? Nineteenth Amendment of the Constitution Bill, 1998' (ARK, 1998). This amendment "allowed the State to consent to be bound by the British-Irish Agreement done at Belfast on 10 April 1998 and provided that certain further amendments to the Constitution, notably to Articles 2 and 3, would come into effect when that agreement entered into force". (Constitution of Ireland, 1994)

[2] The term refers to the period of transition between the election of 1998 and the formal ceding of devolved powers to the NI Assembly in December 1999. In the interim period, the Assembly met to prepare for devolved government.

[3] For example, reports emerged in January 2008 that Ian Paisley Junior, son of the First Minister and himself a Minister in the OFMDFM, had used the negotiations at St Andrews to lobby for and link concessions to constituency matters. (bbc.co.uk 18/01/08)

[4] The complete Northern Ireland (St Andrews Agreement) Bill can be accessed at www.nio.gov.uk.

Chapter 3
The Government of Northern Ireland

The main institutions of government in Northern Ireland are the Assembly and the Executive. In this chapter you will learn about their main roles and how they function. By the end of the chapter you should be able to:

- outline the main roles and functions of the NI Assembly and Executive;
- explain and apply key political concepts in the context of Northern Ireland, such as democracy, power, authority, democratic deficit and power-sharing

GOVERNMENT IN NORTHERN IRELAND takes place through a democratically elected legislative chamber – the Assembly, from which the government, known as the Executive, is formed. It is a unicameral system as there is only one legislative chamber, unlike bicameral models which have two houses of parliament such as Westminster (House of Commons and House of Lords); Republic of Ireland (Dáil and Seanad) or the USA (House of Representatives and Senate). Northern Ireland is not unique in having only one chamber – the other devolved administrations in the UK are also unicameral. In Scotland the legislative chamber is the Scottish Parliament and in Wales it is known as the National Assembly. There are however several features that make the Northern Ireland Assembly and Executive distinct from the other devolved administrations in the UK, not least, the context and circumstances relating to its establishment (emerging after almost thirty years of armed conflict), its history of suspension during its short existence and the electoral mechanisms used to form the Executive and appoint Heads of Committees (the D'Hondt system). These features are considered in this chapter. In the previous chapter the events and circumstances leading to the Good Friday Agreement in 1998 and the establishment of the NI Assembly in

1999 were outlined. It showed how although the GFA continued to provide the basis for government in NI, amendments to it were necessary to enable the Assembly and Executive to operate once more. In this chapter the arrangements for government in Northern Ireland are explored, based on the GFA and the amendments to it in the St Andrews Agreement (2006).

The Northern Ireland Assembly

This agreement provides for a democratically elected Assembly in Northern Ireland which is inclusive in its membership, capable of exercising executive and legislative authority, and subject to safeguards to protect the rights and interests of all sides of the community. *Strand 1, Article 1, The Good Friday Agreement, 1998*

The Northern Ireland Assembly meets in the legislative chamber of Parliament Buildings, Stormont. It was here that the old parliament of NI met until its proroguing in 1972. When it was set up in 1999, the new Assembly was to be qualitatively different from its predecessors. The consociationalist principles enshrined in the GFA were designed to ensure that the composition and voting procedures would make the new Assembly more inclusive and balanced than the parliaments of earlier generations.

> ### Consociationalism
> A form of government which accommodates the diverse interests of divided and plural societies through powersharing in a coalition, made up of parties representing the dominant groups in that society.

The Assembly is made up of 108 members who are elected from the existing 18 Westminster constituencies in Northern Ireland. Six representatives are elected from each constituency. Elected representatives are known as Members of the Legislative Assembly (MLA). The first elections to the new Assembly took place on 25 June 1998 and since then there have been two further Assembly elections (2003 and 2007).

The electoral system used for Assembly elections is Single Transferable Vote (STV), which is a form of proportional representation (PR). This type of electoral system aims to combine constituency representation with proportionality. Northern Ireland's electoral system is explored in Chapter 4.

Under this electoral system the parties with the largest number of votes and consequently seats in the Assembly claim the positions of First Minister and Deputy First Minister respectively. Seats on the NI Executive are allocated on the basis of a party's share of the vote, using a system of electoral allocation known as **D'Hondt**. The positions of Chair and Deputy Chair of the Assembly Committees are also allocated using this system.

The D'Hondt system

This is a system for electoral selection which was devised by a Belgian lawyer, Victor D'Hondt in the nineteenth century. The D'Hondt System (also known as 'highest average method') is based on the principle that seats are won singly and successively on the basis of the highest average. The method requires that the number of seats each party gained in the Assembly be divided initially by one and thereafter by its number of Executive Committee seats plus one (see Appendix 1 for a detailed explanation of the D'Hondt system).

It is through the electoral system that democratic principles are embedded in politics in NI. One of the key principles of democracy is "government of the people, by the people, for the people." In Northern Ireland this is achieved through the Assembly, in which elected representatives are directly elected by voters and from whom the government, or the Executive, is formed. In the NI context, though, it could be argued it is a contested form of democracy.

> The Assembly will exercise *full legislative and executive* authority in respect of those matters currently within the responsibility of the six NI Government departments...
>
> *Strand 1, Article 3, GFA*
>
> The Assembly operating where appropriate on a cross-community basis will be the *prime source of authority* in respect of all devolved responsibilities.
>
> *Strand 1, Article 4, GFA*

Powers of the Assembly

The Good Friday Agreement placed sole responsibility for governing NI with the Northern Ireland Assembly. It is from this Assembly, made up of MLAs from NI's political parties that the government of NI, the Executive Committee, is formed. The Assembly is therefore directly involved in government by nominating Ministers to the government. The Assembly's second crucial role is that of a legislative body: initiating and scrutinising legislation and holding the executive to account in its implementation of this legislation. The NI Assembly is a 'working Assembly' with members actively engaged in the institutions of devolved government.

The Assembly fulfils its legislative role in two ways. Firstly, it meets in full session to debate a motion, vote on legislation or present questions to a minister. The Assembly meets in full, or **plenary** format, on Mondays and Tuesdays. For the remainder of the week MLAs are engaged in a range of activities related to their work in the Assembly, such as participating in committees or in their constituency.

The second way in which the Assembly fulfils its legislative function is through the committee system. It is here, often away from the eyes of media, that the real work of the Assembly takes place.

Business of the Assembly

The Assembly meets on Mondays from 12.00–6.00 pm and Tuesdays from 10.30 am– 6.00 pm. When deciding on the arrangements for the new NI Assembly, it was hoped that the Assembly would keep 'family friendly' hours, unlike Westminster, where parliamentary sessions often run on into the late evening. Debates in the Assembly occasionally overrun the 6.00 pm deadline and can if necessary continue the following day. Emergency sessions of the Assembly can also be called by the Speaker.

To meet in plenary session, there must be at least ten MLAs present (a **quorum**), including the Speaker. If there is not a quorum present, the session is postponed.

The main areas of business conducted by the Assembly are:

- Assembly Business
- Executive Committee Business
- Committee Business
- Questions (Monday 2.30 pm–4.00 pm)
- Private Members' Business
- Private Business
- Adjournment Debates (Tuesday 3.00 pm–6.00 pm)
- Party Business

Source: Standing Order 10, NI Standing Orders of the NI Assembly

---

Adjournment Debates

These are scheduled occasions after the main business of the Assembly has been completed, when individual MLAs may raise any matter, having notified the Speaker of this at least eight days previously.

Standing Order 21, NI Standing Orders of the NI Assembly

The passage of legislation

One of the main functions of the Assembly is to scrutinise and approve legislation. There are various stages in the passage of a Bill. Once a Bill has received legislative approval and is given Royal Assent it becomes an Act. The table opposite shows the different stages.

Voting procedures

The GFA was structured around the need to provide mechanisms for reconciling opposing political interests and so making genuine power-sharing possible. Consequently the GFA addressed the issue of voting procedures in the Assembly in detail.

Stages in the passage of a Bill	
Stage 1	The Bill is introduced to the Assembly with its title read by the Clerk, after having earlier been presented to the Speaker. A copy is sent to the Northern Ireland Human Rights Commission. A Bill can be proposed by a Minister or an MLA.
Stage 2	A general debate on the Bill, with an opportunity for members to vote on its general principles.
Stage 3 (Committee Stage)	Detailed investigation by a committee, followed by a report to the Assembly.
Stage 4 (Consideration Stage)	Consideration of, and an opportunity for members to vote on, the details of the Bill. Including amendments to the proposed Bill.
Stage 5 (Final Stage)	Passing or rejection of the Bill, without further amendment. (The Assembly votes on the Bill.)

The Agreement specified that: "to ensure key decisions are taken on a cross-community basis voting in the Assembly should occur on the basis of either: **parallel consent**, ie a majority of those members present and voting, including a majority of the unionist and nationalist designations present and voting;

(GFA, Strand 1, Article 5 (d) (i))

or a **weighted majority** (60%) of members present and voting, including at least 40% of each of the nationalist and unionist designations present and voting."

(GFA, Strand 1, Article 5 (d) (ii))

A **key decision** is defined as a decision which requires cross-community support and is designated a **key decision** in advance. **Key decisions** include the elections of the Chair of the Assembly, the FM and DFM; standing orders; and budget allocations. Key decisions can also be triggered by a 'petition of concern' brought by a significant minority of Assembly members. Voting on key decisions must take place on a cross-community basis using either Parallel Consent or Weighted Majority.

Parallel consent in effect means that when the Assembly votes on a motion the result is determined by the overall majority, which must include a majority of self designated unionists and nationalists. A **weighted majority** means that there must be 60% of the members present and voting and at least 40% of those voting should be both unionist and nationalists.

These two mechanisms were built into the GFA to safeguard against **majoritarianism** on strategic issues. While the intention behind these two mechanisms was to promote genuine powersharing, they can also be viewed as anti democratic instruments, which discriminate against the minor political parties in the Assembly. This became apparent in autumn 2001 during the crisis over the election of the FM and DFM. The Northern Ireland's Women's Coalition designated one of its members as unionist, but this was not enough to secure the crucial vote. In the event, it fell to the Alliance Party to redesignate three of its members but the party agreed to this only after extracting the promise of a review of the voting procedures in the Assembly.

The malleability of the system and its potential abuse, particularly in relation to the designation and redesignation of political parties, underlined the need for change and this was addressed at the St Andrews talks with a proposal in relation to community designation which would involve an amendment to the 1998 Act to provide that an Assembly Member would not be able to change community designation for the whole of an Assembly term except in the case of a change of membership of political party (St Andrews Agreement online).

The role of the Speaker

Most legislative chambers are headed by a presiding officer, often referred to as the **Speaker**. In the Northern Ireland Assembly the Speaker manages the day-to-day running of the legislative chamber: scheduling debates, overseeing question time and managing plenary sessions of the Assembly. They deal with issues of procedure and order in the chamber and their ruling is final. The speaker is assisted in their work by three deputies (NI Assembly, Standing Orders 4 and 5).

The Speaker is elected by MLAs at the first session of a new Assembly (ie every four years, following elections to the Assembly). This election must be held within eight days of the poll. The Speaker is elected by the special cross-community voting procedures and holds office for the lifetime of that Assembly *(NI Assembly, Standing Orders 4 and 5).*

The Speaker of the first NI Assembly was Lord Alderdice, former leader of APNI. However, he was not elected to the post but was instead appointed by the Secretary of State prior to the first meeting of the Assembly in shadow mode in July 1998. This appointment was seen as necessary to give leadership and guidance to a new and relatively inexperienced Assembly at a time when many important decisions would be required. Lord Alderdice retained the post of Speaker until his resignation in 2004. In 2006, while the Assembly was still formally suspended, Eileen Bell was appointed as Speaker of the Transitional Assembly. She was the first woman and first Catholic to be appointed as Speaker *(bbc.co.uk, 10 April 2006).*

Speakers of Northern Ireland Assembly

	Speaker	Deputy Speakers
2007	William Hay (DUP)	John Dallat (SDLP) David McClarty (UUP) Francie Molloy (SF)
2006	Eileen Bell (Alliance) Interim Speaker	Francie Molloy (SF) Jim Wells (DUP)
1998 – 2004	Lord Alderdice (Alliance)	Sir John Gorman (UUP) (Feb 2000 - Feb 2002) Donovan McCelland (SDLP) appointed Feb 2000 Jane Morrice (NIWC) appointed Feb 2000 Jim Wilson (UUP) appointed Feb 2002

Source: NI Assembly Education Service & bbc.co.uk

The committee system

When the Assembly meets in plenary form, ie full session, it is the prime source of legislative authority on devolved matters. However, much of the day-to-day work of the Assembly takes place at the committee level. Assembly committees are also known as **Statutory Committees** and in essence are small working groups of members, created to cope with the volume of business in the house.

The GFA specified that the: "Committees will have a scrutiny, policy development and consultation role with respect to the Department with which each is associated and will have a role in initiation of legislation." *(GFA, Strand 1, Article 9)*

The GFA designated their specific responsibility to:

"consider and advise on Departmental budgets and Annual Plans in the context of the overall budget allocation;

approve relevant secondary legislation and take the Committee stage of relevant primary legislation;

call for persons and papers;

initiate enquiries and make reports;

consider and advise on matters brought to the Committee by its Minister."

(GFA, Strand 1, Article 9)

The GFA envisaged that the committee system would promote the power-sharing philosophy in two ways: firstly membership of committees was decided using the D'Hondt system to ensure that committee representation is commensurate with seats in the Assembly; and secondly that the committees would work in partnership with each of their target departments.

Each committee is made up of 11 members drawn from the full spectrum of political parties represented in the Assembly. Decisions within committees are reached on the basis of a simple majority. Committee members are allocated in proportion to the relative strengths of the parties in the Assembly. The Chairs and Deputy Chairs of Committees are also allocated by D'Hondt in such a manner that they are not drawn from the same party as that of the relevant minister. The table below demonstrates how this operated in the Assembly elected in May 2007.

Table 5 *Committee Leadership in NI Assembly 2007*

Committee	Chair of Committee	Deputy Chair of Committee	Minister of Executive Department
Agricultural	Dr William McCrea (DUP)	Tom Elliot (UUP)	Michelle Gildernew (SF)
Culture, Arts and Leisure	Barry McElduff (SF)	David McNarry (UUP)	Edwin Poots (DUP)
Education	Sammy Wilson (DUP)	Dominic Bradley (SDLP)	Catriona Ruane (SF)
Enterprise, Trade and Investment	Mark Durkan (SDLP)	Paul Maskey (SF)	Nigel Dodds (UUP)
Environment	Patsy McGlone (SDLP)	Cathal Boylan (SF)	Arlene Foster (DUP)
Finance and Personnel	Mitchel McLaughlin (SF)	Mervyn Storey (DUP)	Peter Robinson (DUP)
Employment and Learning (previously Higher and Further Education, Training and Employment)	Sue Ramsey (SF)	Jimmy Spratt (DUP)	Reg Empey (UUP)
Health, Social Services and Public Safety	Iris Robinson (DUP)	Michelle O'Neill (SF)	Michael McGimpsey (UUP)
Regional Development	Fred Cobain (UUP)	Jim Wells (DUP)	Conor Murphy (SF)
Social Development	Gregory Campbell (DUP)	David Hilditch (DUP)	Margaret Ritchie (SDLP)

The manner in which the principle of proportionality is applied to Assembly committees is highlighted by the example below from the Education Committee in the Assembly elected in May 2007.

Functions of the committees

Table 6 NI Assembly Election 2007 – Party Seats

Political Party	2007
Democratic Unionist Party	36
Sinn Féin	28
Ulster Unionist Party	18
Social Democratic and Labour Party	16
Alliance Party	7
Others	3
Total	**108**

Table 7 Membership of Assembly Education Committee (2007)

Political Party	Number of seats on Committee
Democratic Unionist Party	4
Sinn Féin	2
Ulster Unionist Party	2
Social Democratic and Labour Party	2
Alliance Party	1
Total	**11**

Source: Northern Ireland Assembly website.

According to GFA, the main purpose of the committees is to advise and assist departments in the formulation of policy. They exist to scrutinise their subject departments, advise them on policy and can exercise the power to initiate legislation within their subject areas. The example on page 38, from a meeting of the Agriculture Committee held in July 2007, shows how an Assembly Committee undertakes its role in advising and assisting in the formulation of policy.

In this example, the Minister for the Environment has attended a meeting of the Environment Committee to brief committee members on a new piece of legalisation, the Climate Change Bill. Committee members were able to question the Minister about this. The committee agreed to discuss and prepare its response to the new Bill, and the Minister agreed to respond to this. The exchange of information between the Minister and her department and the Committee was also agreed. The discussion between the Minister and the Committee, and the agreement to work collaboratively and share information, reflects the principle of partnership between Executive and Legislature which underpinned the GFA.

Committees can call for persons and papers. This may involve calling a specialist in the committee's area of interest to meet with the committee. Committees can also initiate enquiries and make reports.

COMMITTEE FOR THE ENVIRONMENT
MINUTES OF PROCEEDINGS
THURSDAY 5 July 2007

[Extract from Minutes]

Agenda item 3
Climate Change Bill – Legislative Consent Motion (Sewell)

- The Minister, Arlene Foster, briefed the Members on the Climate Change Bill.
- The Minister answered questions from the Members.
- The Minister, Arlene Foster, briefed the Members on the Review of Public Administration.
- The Minister answered questions from the Members.
- Agreed – Committee to provide response on Climate Bill to Minister by October 2007.
- Agreed – Minister to respond to Committee.
- Agreed – Committee to send copy of response to Climate Change Coalition NI for their comments on questions.
- Agreed – Department to provide Committee with briefing on 'emerging findings' by the end of September 2007.
- Agreed – Minister to provide Committee with an early sight of recommendations.

Source: Environment Committee Minutes, 5 July 2007

How effective are Assembly committees?

The consociationalist nature of the NI Assembly and Executive means that in NI there is no formal opposition. The role of scrutinising and challenging executive decisions has fallen to the committees and in this capacity the committees can be quite effective. One political observer noted that "a truce characterises the work of committees, both statutory and standing: enquiries are conducted, policies analysed; legislation is scrutinised and reports produced all in a largely business-like fashion" (www.ucl.ac.uk/constitution-unit/monrep/ni/nimay01.pdf, Nations and Regions, May 2001:26).

However, this was not always the case and there have been cases of differences between the Assembly Committee and the Minister of the Department. For example in 2000, the Minister for Health, Bairbre de Brún, differed with both the Health Committee and the Assembly over the location of maternity services in Belfast. More recently, tensions surfaced between the Minister of Education, Catriona Ruane, and the Education Committee in relation to the future arrangements for the replacement of the Eleven Plus examination.

Other Assembly committees

In addition to the statutory committees linked to government departments, there are a number of other committees within the Assembly. These are known as **Standing Committees** and their main work is concerned with the business and operation of the Assembly and Legislature.

Standing Committee	Function
Assembly and Executive Review Committee	Consider matters relating to the functioning of the Assembly or the Executive Committee as may be referred to it by the Assembly.
Committee on Procedures	Consider and review on an ongoing basis the Standing Orders and procedures of the Assembly.
Business Committee	To make arrangements for the business of the Assembly.
Public Accounts Committee	Consider accounts, and reports on accounts laid before the Assembly.
Committee on Standards and Privileges	Committee has been established to consider specific matters relating to privilege referred to it by the Assembly.
Audit Committee	To exercise the functions laid upon the Assembly by Section 66 of the Northern Ireland Act 1998.

Source: Northern Ireland Assembly (The Assembly Committees)

The role and function of the MLA

For the Assembly and its committees to function as intended, much depends on the Assembly Members, the MLAs. Most MLAs have become professional politicians and this requires juggling a range of activities and commitments. MLAs attend the plenary sessions of the Assembly on Mondays and Tuesdays. Wednesdays and Thursdays are set aside for committee meetings – such meetings can last for two or three hours and most members sit on at least two committees. On Fridays most MLAs aim to devote time to constituency work. In addition to this schedule, MLAs attend other meetings such as those with lobby groups, foreign visitors or with members of other political parties in NI. The itinerary on page 40 represents how one MLA spent a day.

This busy itinerary shows the demands an MLA faces in the course of a day, trying to reconcile their actual work in the Assembly and its committees, with meeting the demands of their constituents. This is an area no MLA can afford to neglect: just as they were voted in, so they can be voted out. Some MLAs argue that the daily demands and pressures of the position of elected representative more than justifies the annual

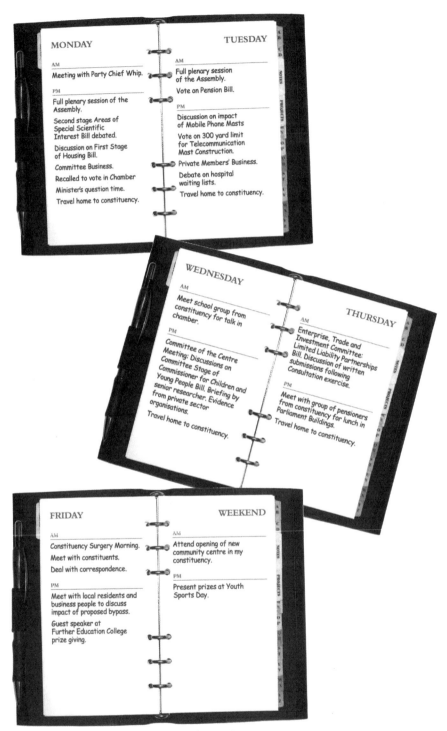

MONDAY

AM

Meeting with Party Chief Whip.

PM

Full plenary session of the Assembly.

Second stage Areas of Special Scientific Interest Bill debated.

Discussion on First Stage of Housing Bill.

Committee Business.

Recalled to vote in Chamber

Minister's question time.

Travel home to constituency.

TUESDAY

AM

Full plenary session of the Assembly.

Vote on Pension Bill.

PM

Discussion on impact of Mobile Phone Masts

Vote on 300 yard limit for Telecommunication Mast Construction.

Private Members' Business.

Debate on hospital waiting lists.

Travel home to constituency.

WEDNESDAY

AM

Meet school group from constituency for talk in chamber.

PM

Committee of the Centre Meeting: Discussions on Committee Stage of Commissioner for Children and Young People Bill. Briefing by senior researcher. Evidence from private sector organisations.

Travel home to constituency.

THURSDAY

AM

Enterprise, Trade and Investment Committee: Limited Liability Partnerships Bill. Discussion of written submissions following Consultation exercise.

PM

Meet with group of pensioners from constituency for lunch in Parliament Buildings.

Travel home to constituency.

FRIDAY

AM

Constituency Surgery Morning.

Meet with constituents.

Deal with correspondence.

PM

Meet with local residents and business people to discuss impact of proposed bypass.

Guest speaker at Further Education College prize giving.

WEEKEND

AM

Attend opening of new community centre in my constituency.

PM

Present prizes at Youth Sports Day.

Source: http://education.niassembly.gov.uk/information/diary.htm

salary of £41,321 (plus expenses), though this is comparably lower than for elected representatives elsewhere in the UK. For example, the salary for a Welsh MWA[1] is £46,191; for Scottish MSPs[2], £52,226 and for Westminster MPs, £60,227 (*Belfast Telegraph*, 1 February 2007). Northern Ireland's MLAs continued to receive their salaries and expenses during the period that the Assembly was suspended. However, in 2006, the NI Secretary of State linked MLA salaries to the need to find a way out from the political deadlock of recent years (NIO, 8 January 2006).

Composition of the Northern Ireland Assembly

Northern Ireland is a largely homogeneous, albeit polarised society[3] and this is reflected in the composition of the Assembly. The 2007 Assembly consists of 108 MLAs and of these 18 (or 16.7%) are women. This is the same number as the 2003 election. In fact there were fewer women candidates for this election than for the 1998 and 2003 Assembly elections. This is in spite of the fact that legislation exists in Northern Ireland to encourage greater participation by women in public life (Centre for Advancement of Women in Politics: 2007). In general, however, women are under-represented in public life in NI; they comprise around one third of public appointees but only one quarter of chairs of public bodies (Wilford, Wilson & Claussen, 2007:8). In 2003, the Northern Ireland Women's Coalition, formed in 1996 to contest elections to the Northern Ireland Forum, and operating on the principles of inclusion, accommodation, human rights and equity with a cross community focus, lost both seats that it had won in the 1998 election. Arguably this was the result of the narrowing of the political centre and the squeeze on smaller political parties as the polarisation between and within the unionist and nationalist camps became more acute. However, in a male dominated political context, the NIWC played an important role in highlighting and lobbying on behalf of women and other marginalised groups in NI. In 2005 the party's offices were closed and in 2006 the party was formally wound down. One if its founder members, Monica McWilliams, was appointed Northern Ireland's Human Rights Commissioner in 2005 (bbc.co.uk, 16 June 2005)

A significant breakthrough occurred in the 2007 elections when Anna Lo (APNI) was elected as first MLA from an ethnic minority (bbc.co.uk, 9 March 2007) There were 25 nationalities registered to vote in the election in 2007, with 6,200 migrants from EU countries on the electoral register at that time. While Anna Lo's election was an important milestone, the Assembly elected in 2007 was made up predominantly of white males.

The Northern Ireland Executive

The Good Friday Agreement provided for a "democratically elected Assembly in Northern Ireland which is inclusive in its membership, **capable of exercising executive and legislative authority...**"   *GFA, Strand 1, Article 1*

In this respect the Assembly fulfils two roles, that of a legislative chamber, and that of forming the government, known in Northern Ireland as **the Executive.**

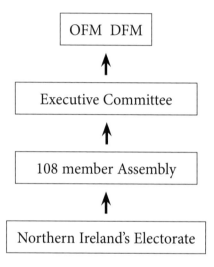

The government or Executive in NI is formed by and from the Assembly 'by reference to the number of seats each party has in the Assembly' (*GFA, Strand 1, Article 16*). This means that the party with the largest numbers of seats in the Assembly will be able to claim the largest number of ministerial posts.

For example, in the 2007 Assembly elections, the DUP formed the largest party in the Assembly with 36 seats. In the Executive it was allocated four Ministerial posts. Sinn Féin, which came second with 28 Assembly seats, was allocated three Ministerial posts. Parties such as the UUP and SDLP, which had held the greatest number of Ministerial posts in the Executive formed after the 1998 election, were allocated only one to two Ministerial posts after the 2007 elections. This is illustrated in Table 8 opposite.

Ministers are not elected by the Assembly but allocated to their posts by their parties through the D'Hondt system. There are ten Ministers for the ten government departments in NI. These Ministers constitute the Executive Committee. This committee is headed by a First Minister (FM) and Deputy First Minister (DFM).

Table 8 *Allocation of posts in NI Executive Committee, 2007*

Executive Department	Minister	Political Party Affiliation	No of Executive Seats	No of Assembly Seats
Culture, Arts and Leisure	Edwin Poots	DUP	4	36
Environment	Arlene Foster			
Enterprise, Trade and Investment	Nigel Dodds			
Finance and Personnel	Peter Robinson			
Agriculture	Michelle Gildernew	SF	3	28
Education	Catriona Ruane			
Regional Development	Conor Murphy			
Employment and Learning	Reg Empey	UUP	2	18
Health, Social Services and Public Safety	Michael McGimpsey			
Social Development	Margaret Ritchie	SDLP	1	16

The role of FM and DFM

> The FM and DFM are "jointly elected into office by the Assembly voting on a cross community basis according to parallel consent". *GFA, Strand 1, Article 15.*
>
> Their role is to convene and preside over the Executive Committee *(Article 17)* and "their duties will include, *inter alia*, dealing with and coordinating the work of the Executive Committee and the response of the NI administration to external relationships" (Article 18).

The FM and DFM are essentially the chief executives or heads of government in the EC. They have central responsibility for a range of functions including equality, economic policy, community relations and liaison with the North/South Ministerial Council (NSMC) and the British-Irish Council (BIC). They coordinate and chair the weekly meetings of the EC, having previously agreed the agenda. Underpinning the power-sharing philosophy of the GFA, a built-in safeguard ensures that the FM and DFM must be elected jointly (*Strand 2, Article 15*) – one cannot remain in office without the other. In this respect the roles of FM and DFM have equality of status, creating what some commentators have called a 'dyarchy'.

In the first Assembly following the GFA, the posts of FM and DFM were taken by David Trimble (UUP) and Seamus Mallon (SDLP) respectively. In November 2001 Seamus Mallon resigned as DFM and stepped aside as deputy leader of the SDLP. He was replaced as DFM by Mark Durkan.

Following the elections in March 2007 and the reconvening of the Assembly, Ian Paisley and Martin McGuinness were elected as First Minister and Deputy First Minister respectively.

The NI Executive		
	Office of First and Deputy First Minister (OFMDFM)	
	First Minister	**Deputy First Minister**
2008	Peter Robinson (DUP) May 2008 – Ian Paisley (DUP) May 2007–June 2008	Martin McGuinness (SF)
2007	**OFMDFM Junior Ministers** Gerry Kelly (SF) Jeffrey Donaldson (DUP) Feb 2008 – Ian Paisley Jnr (DUP) May 2007 – Feb 2008	
1999–2002	David Trimble (UUP)	Seamus Mallon (SDLP) Mark Durkan (SDLP)

Executive Power and Authority

Devolved government means that a regional government is given autonomy to govern and legislate on key issues, while central government retains jurisdiction over a number of areas, such as security. In NI, the powers transferred or devolved to the NI Executive and Assembly deal with finance and personnel, agriculture, education, culture and the arts, health, social services, economic and regional development and environment.

It is important to note the distinction between devolution and federalism. Under a devolved administration the transferred powers can be taken back. This has occurred in NI on four occasions since 1999: two long periods of suspension of devolution (February–May 2000 and from October 2002) and two one day suspensions in 2001.

The government at Westminster retains jurisdiction over a number of areas of government in NI. These are known as excepted and reserved matters and include matters such as policing, security policy, prisons, criminal justice, international relations, taxation, national insurance, regulation of financial services and the regulation of telecommunications and broadcasting. The Secretary of State (SoSNI) and the NIO are responsible for overseeing these areas.

The Executive at work

The Executive is effectively the government of NI. It is essentially a cabinet government and its main purpose is to meet and decide on the major questions of government for NI.

> The GFA charged the EC with providing:
>
> "… a forum for the discussion of, and agreement on, issues which cut across the responsibilities of two or more Ministers, for prioritising executive and legislative proposals and for recommending a common position where necessary."
>
> *(GFA, Strand 2, Article 19)*
>
> It is also the remit of the EC to agree on a yearly basis, and review when necessary, a programme for government which incorporates a budget and which is brought before the Assembly for its approval. *(Article 20)*

When the Assembly is in session and not in suspension, the Executive Committee meets on a weekly basis, but the FM and DFM can convene additional meetings to deal with urgent matters. A typical meeting might consist of addressing matters arising, a discussion on budgetary matters, a paper presented by a minister on a matter of concern and discussion on future legislative matters.[4]

One of the first tasks of the Executive Committee on coming to power is to reach agreement on a draft Programme for Government. In January 2008, the FM and DFM outlined their new Programme of Government to the Assembly. The Programme for Government outlines the government's priorities for the next three years. These included:

- increasing the employment rate from 70% to 75% by 2020;
- creating a minimum of 6,500 jobs, 85% of which will be above the private sector median wage;
- ensuring that 68% of school leavers achieve at least 5 GCSEs at Grade C or above;
- reducing the number of children killed on the roads by 50% by 2012;
- providing free public transport to everyone aged 60 or above;
- investing over £500 million in regenerating disadvantaged communities by 2012;
- ensuring that by 2009 no one will wait longer than nine weeks for an outpatient appointment, nine weeks for a diagnostic test and 17 weeks for treatment; and
- by 2025 reduce greenhouse gas emissions by 25% below 1990 levels.

In addressing the Assembly in relation to the Programme for Government, the DFM observed that:

"At long last local Ministers are making decisions on behalf of local people. The programme we have laid before the Assembly today has been debated, agreed and endorsed by local Ministers." (NIO, 2008)

The DFM's statement gives an insight into how the Executive operates and reaches its decisions: debating, agreeing and endorsing proposals. These are then presented to the Assembly for scrutiny and approval.

In this respect the Executive and Assembly are operating in the way envisaged in the GFA and the 'democratic deficit' which existed in NI under direct rule, may be beginning to be reduced. During the Assembly debate on the Programme for Government, one MLA commented that:

"It is reassuring for the people of Northern Ireland that they can clearly see where we want to take this Province. That stands in stark contrast to the days of Labour 'fly-in' Ministers who had little, if any, drive to build a strong and competitive Northern Ireland economy" (Official Report, 28 January 2008).

Collective government but not collective responsibility?

The meeting of the first Executive Committee of the new Northern Ireland Assembly on 2 December 1999 was an historic occasion. The government, which was to administer Northern Ireland, had been established on a genuinely inclusive basis. All major political parties in NI were represented in government for the first time and Northern Ireland politicians would be making decisions about Northern Ireland affairs for the first time in over thirty years. Despite the symbolic importance of the occasion, the formation of the Executive Committee also represented a challenge for those Ministers who formed it and for the parties that had nominated them. The challenge was to set aside party political differences in government, work collectively to govern NI, and oversee progress and development in all aspects of life. Ultimately, the inability to resolve party political differences brought the first Assembly to suspension and resulted in the restoration of Direct Rule.

The Executive could be described as a form of coalition government in that it is made up of a number of different parties. However, the coalition is not formed out of political expediency or horse-trading but rather on the consociationalist principles embedded in the GFA. The Executive could also be described as a form of cabinet government, but again, it does not operate as a cabinet government usually operates, headed by a President or Prime Minister and made of one political party or more if it is a coalition. In this respect while the Executive has elements of coalition and cabinet government, it is not founded on either of these.

The GFA envisaged that decisions within the EC would be reached collectively. This was not the case in the first EC (1999–2002). DUP Ministers refused to participate in the weekly meetings of the full Executive because of the presence of SF in government. This meant that when the Executive met, not all Ministers were present. The DUP conducted its business with the EC Committee via correspondence, and while the party claimed that this enabled its Ministers to fulfil their Ministerial commitments, clearly it was not a satisfactory arrangement.

One criticism of the first Executive Committee is that while it may have achieved collective government, collective responsibility was lacking. The principle of collective responsibility underpins the working of cabinet government. Collective responsibility obliges all ministers to 'sing the same song' on the grounds that they are collectively responsible to, and removable by, parliament. Individual responsibility holds that ministers are personally responsible to parliament for departmental blunders or policy failures (Heywood, 2000;146).

While NI ministers appeared to embrace the idea of individual responsibility, there was little evidence of collective responsibility. This can be explained by the nature of the EC, which is an involuntary coalition. Normally in cabinet government one party dominates or where a coalition government has emerged, a common course and plan for government has been agreed. Cabinet government and collective decision-making operate on the basis of a degree of unity and a set of common aims. The NI Executive is made up of ministers assigned to the Executive Committee by their respective party through a method of power-sharing designed to ensure that all dominant parties are represented. The NI Executive has been hindered by the reality that the more parties there are in government, the more difficult it can be to achieve consensus. The other reality is that the EC lacks ideological cohesion. While there may be agreement on socio-economic issues, the parties have disagreed on how NI should be governed. The absence of a common goal or vision, or differences in what that goal should be, seriously impeded progress for the first Executive Committee and Assembly. The GFA was criticised for institutionalising the nationalist-unionist conflict, rather than developing a new multi-cultural constitutional option (Wilson, 2001:77)

This was seen as the result of the consociational model on which the NI Assembly and Executive is based. In this model the ideal is elite domination of the common 'pillars', ie government departments, with minimum contact between heads of departments (ministers) and so less opportunity for conflict. The elites are insulated from wider accountability and so better able to take the decisions needed (Wilford and Wilson, 2001:42). The consequence of this was that the NI Assembly was "executive dominant" rather than "legislature led" (Wilford and Wilson, 2001:3).

Mindful of these weaknesses in the original agreement (GFA), and acutely aware of the need to clearly define executive roles and responsibilities, the architects of the St Andrews Agreement (2006) sought to address this. They did this by explicating the Ministerial Code of Conduct. There were two strategies evident: one designed to prevent unilateral actions by Ministers and the other to secure full participation in all institutions of the GFA.

The GFA afforded Ministers the opportunity to bypass the Assembly and its Committees by requiring them only to "liaise regularly with their committee" (Article 22) and granting Ministers "full executive authority in their respective areas of responsibility, within any broad programme agreed by the Executive Committee and endorsed by the Assembly as a whole" (Article 24). During the term of first Executive Committee, the actions of the Health Minister and the decision by the Education Minister to suspend the Eleven Plus had highlighted the opportunity for Ministers to act unilaterally.

In the reconstituted Assembly, the St Andrews Agreement sought to reduce the risk of Ministers acting unilaterally by requiring "all Ministers or Junior Ministers to act in accordance with the provisions of the Ministerial Code" (St Andrews Agreement 28A:I) and by making provision that:

"Ministerial decisions can be deferred to the Executive Committee if petitioned by 30 members of the Assembly, if a ministerial decision may have been taken in contravention of the Ministerial Code or if it relates to a matter of public importance". (28 B:1)

The functioning of the first Executive Committee had also been constrained by the refusal of DUP Ministers to collaborate in government with Ministers from SF and to participate in institutions such as the North South Ministerial Council. Although many of the DUP's objections to participation in government with SF have been lessened in the years since the Assembly's suspension, nevertheless the St Andrews Agreement sought to make explicit and accountable ministerial participation in all aspects of government in NI. This was specified in a revised Ministerial Pledge of Office which included a commitment to:

"promote the interest of the whole community; to participate fully in the Executive Committee, NSMC and BIC; to uphold the rule of law; and endorsing and supporting of the PSNI and criminal justice system and institutions including the Policing Board."

This was further underlined by the statement in the St Andrews Agreement that:

"It shall be a Ministerial responsibility of each appropriate Minister or if a Minister or junior minister is nominated to attend a meeting of the NSMC or BIC to participate in the meeting so far as it relates to matters for which the appropriate Minister has responsibility" (52B:1).

During its first term of office (1999–2003), the EC withstood many crises. Contentious issues such as decommissioning, prisoner releases, and reform of the RUC, dominated politics within and outside the NI Assembly. The suspension of the Assembly at various times between 2000 and 2002 impaired continuity in policy-making and decision-making in the government departments. The ministers who were appointed to the first EC were relatively inexperienced in their posts and few had served in a government capacity before. Consequently the first phase of devolution represented a steep learning curve for most ministers.

In spite of these difficulties, the first EC succeeded in acting together to produce a Programme for Government and a budget. It acted collectively and presented a united front on policy when necessary. Individual ministers embraced their ministerial brief and worked hard to develop the areas of interest of their department.

The prolonged period of suspension from October 2002–May 2007 provided ample time to reflect on the weaknesses of the GFA and to identify specific areas for clarification and elaboration. The St Andrews Agreement sought to address these and to provide a more secure foundation for the restoration of devolved government.

Summary

The convening of the first NI Assembly was an historic event in Northern Ireland. It marked the restoration of democratic politics and an end to the sectarianism and violence of the past. At that time, many doubted the effectiveness of the Assembly and predicted, accurately, its collapse. The first Assembly withstood many crises and was forced to conduct its business against a backdrop of violence, punishment shootings and beatings, and sectarian murders. However, it survived in spite of this and undertook its business in a serious and professional manner. For all involved, the early years of the Assembly were a learning experience and in spite of the difficulties, progress was made, legislation passed and a commitment to strengthening democracy and democratic institutions in NI continued to grow.

In the restored Assembly of May 2007, perhaps the will to succeed was even greater. The alternatives, for politicians and citizens, are well understood: return to conflict or return to direct rule. Neither option is preferable to all stakeholders in NI, including the NI political parties, the British government and the Irish government.

Yet in its initial phase, the restored Assembly and Executive have surpassed all expectations. The relationship between the FM and DFM (Ian Paisley and Martin McGuinness) extended beyond good rapport and *bon amie* and reflected a commitment to work in the interests of Northern Ireland and its citizens. There was a discernible will to 'make it work' in spite of changes in leadership.

Notes

[1] MWA – Member of the Welsh Assembly

[2] MSP – Member of the Scottish Parliament

[3] The last census for Northern was conducted in 2001 with the next one scheduled for 2011. Consequently this does not capture the increase in the number of migrant workers since 2004. The number of National Insurance Numbers (NINos) issued by the NIO gives some indication of the scale of this. For example in 2004 –2005, 5,826 were issued to non UK nationals. Of this, 752 were Poles. In 2005-06, the number of NINos issued increased to 15,614, of which 5,460 were issued to Polish nationals (DSE, 2007, NISRA, 2008, Table 1.12 NINo). According to the 2001 census, the population of Northern Ireland was 1,685,267. (www.nisra.gov.uk, accessed 29 April 2008)

[4] The business of the EC can be seen in the News Releases which follow meetings of the Executive: www.northernireland.gov.uk/news.htm

Chapter 4
The Northern Ireland Political Parties

The policies and strategies of Northern Ireland's political parties have played an important role in determining and shaping how Northern Ireland is governed. In this chapter you will learn how NI's political parties have adapted to devolved government and how the NI electorate has responded to the altered political context in Northern Ireland since the GFA.

By the end of the chapter you will be able to:

- outline the role of political parties and the strategies and policies of the main NI political parties;

- analyse how the strategies and policies of the main NI political parties have changed since 1994; and

- assess how and why electoral support for the main political parties has changed since 1994.

NORTHERN IRELAND COULD BE described as a multi-party state in that there are a number of political parties for voters to choose from. However these parties tend to stem from the two main blocs that characterise politics in Northern Ireland – Unionist and Nationalist. Smaller political parties, especially cross community parties, exist in the very narrow political centre. As a result of changes to party policy and strategy, dominant political parties such as the UUP and SDLP have been supplanted by their more radical counterparts: DUP and SF. The electoral success of the DUP and SF reflected the positive response from voters to changes in strategy by these parties and forced the UUP and SDLP into a period of review and reform of party performance. Unlike many other political parties and political leaders, NI's political parties have all played a central role in delivering 'the peace' in Northern Ireland that took over a decade to agree. In this sense, NI's political parties had an additional responsibility, as well as those usually associated with political parties, in liberal democratic, multi-party states.

The role of political parties

In representative democracies, political parties fulfil a number of roles including:

- representation
- mediation
- governing

One of the most important roles of political parties is to represent the electorate.

Elected representatives of political parties are usually elected by voters who support their policies, though sometimes electors vote tactically to prevent another party or politician getting votes. Political parties also mediate between the electorate and the government, working in the interests of their supporters and safeguarding those interests if they are at risk. Political parties can also form the government. In majoritarian systems such as the UK parliament, the political party with the largest number of MPs elected will form the government, though if it is a narrow majority, it may be necessary to form a coalition government with one or more political parties. In other polities, where proportional electoral systems are used, coalition governments tend to occur more frequently, though the four party Executive in Northern Ireland is more unusual.

The existence of political parties and their role in political debate and decision-making is usually a measure of the extent to which a society can be described as **pluralist** and a range of diverse views are represented on the political spectrum.

Political Parties in Northern Ireland

There are a number of ways in which the role of political parties in Northern Ireland differs from those of other liberal democratic states. NI's political parties operate in a *post conflict* context. The ending of the conflict in NI was made possible by shifts in traditional ideological positions held by key parties. Part of the challenge for NI's political parties has been to deal with the legacy of these historic positions in such a way that they are able to move forward in a new context.

Another difference is the narrowness of the political centre in Northern Ireland. Previously this narrow centre was occupied by cross community parties such as the Alliance Party and the Northern Ireland Women's Coalition. However, in successive elections since the GFA, the centre has been squeezed further – the NIWC has dissolved itself – though support for the APNI has remained more constant. The traditional model of party affiliation on a left-right political spectrum is less applicable in NI. The political process revolves around two blocs – Unionist and Nationalist, and there is a wide spectrum of opinion even within these blocs. In the past in NI, politics has been dominated by the drive to reconcile differences between and within the two blocs.

In this context, NI's party system is noteworthy on several counts. Firstly, the presence of two dominant political blocs has resulted in a small political centre in NI.

Secondly, parties tend to compete within blocs for votes rather than between blocs. Thirdly, minor political parties have limited influence and limited opportunity for influence because of the dominance of the major parties and because of the voting procedures for the NI Assembly established in the GFA.

The successful implementation of the GFA and devolved government for NI depended upon the support of all NI's major political parties. Since most of the parties were involved in the negotiating process, it was incumbent upon them to support the final package. Most of the parties therefore backed the GFA and the institutions it proposed, though not necessarily working with other political parties, such as the DUP's refusal to work with SF in the first NI Assembly.

One of the most significant developments since the GFA Agreement has been the shift in support from the parties that have dominated constitutional politics – UUP and SDLP – to the parties that in the past have been diametrically opposed to each other, DUP and SF. So dramatic has the shift in support been, that the DUP and SF became the two largest parties in the NI Assembly after the 2007 Assembly Elections and so were entitled to take the posts of First Minister and Deputy First Minister.

This altered political landscape was due in part to the changing policies and strategies adopted by the main political parties in Northern Ireland which are explored in the following section.

The Ulster Unionist Party (UUP)

In some respects the Ulster Unionist Party became one of the victims of the changed political context in Northern Ireland after the GFA. The party had played a central role in the peace process and in securing the Agreement in 1998. The party won 26 seats in the first elections to the Assembly in 1998 and the party leader, David Trimble, became the First Minister of the 'New Northern Ireland Assembly.' However in the implementation of the agreement and the operation of government, the party became unstuck. This could be attributed to growing opposition from within the party at the leadership's resolve to remain in government with SF, in the absence of full, unilateral and verifiable decommissioning of weapons. The UUP's role as the traditional voice of constitutional unionism was rapidly challenged by the DUP and to a lesser extent by the minor unionist parties such as the PUP and UKUP, which manifested in the seepage of voters and the decamping of politicians from the UUP to the DUP.

The ousting of the UUP from its place as the Unionist party of government was a blow for a party that had dominated politics in NI for much of the 20th century. The historic origins of the UUP lie in the creation of the Ulster Unionist Council (UUC) in 1905 with a specific aim to prevent Home Rule. The first Unionist leader, Colonel Saunderson, was elected as the member for the North Armagh constituency in 1885, twenty years before the creation of the UUP, at a time when politics in both Britain and Ireland was increasingly polarised by the Home Rule issue. Encouraged by an active campaign led by CS Parnell and the Irish Parliamentary Party (IPP), the sympathetic

Liberal PM, Gladstone, proposed Home Rule Bills in 1886 and 1893. As Home Rule began to look increasingly likely, Unionist MPs orchestrated a resistance campaign, both at Westminster and within Ulster. When the Third Home Rule Bill emerged in 1912, Ulster Unionists, now led by Edward Carson, prepared for armed resistance to self-government for Ireland. Carson had accepted the need for the use of force and sanctioned the organisation of the Ulster Volunteer Force (UVF).

The intervention of WWI and the Republican Rising in Dublin in 1916 radically altered the shape of Irish politics, and by 1920 a revised Home Rule Bill, in the form of the Government of Ireland Act, became law. This Act provided for the creation of a new NI state and granted it self-government. In the founding elections for the new NI Parliament (May 1921), the UUP secured an overwhelming victory and Sir James Craig, the party leader, became the first PM of NI.

The union with Britain had been retained but Northern Ireland now had its own government and parliament. The unionist electoral majority ensured that the UUP would become the party of government and this was the case from 1921 until the proroguing of the NI parliament in 1972.

In the new Parliament for NI, meeting initially and temporarily in the Presbyterian Theological College building in Belfast, the Unionist Party won 40 of the 52 seats in the House of Commons. It was a majority which the Unionists were able to maintain for much of the history of the NI parliament: in the elections in 1969, the Unionist Party won 36 of the 52 seats, securing 48.2% share of the vote.

The UUP retained its governing and electoral hegemony in NI until 1972. The proposed power-sharing Assembly to be established in 1974 signalled the end of the UUP as the natural party of government and the necessity for the party to adapt itself to power-sharing with nationalist parties in NI.

This represented a huge challenge for the party and confronted with the need to engage in the politics of accommodation and to recognise the need for an 'Irish dimension', the party factionalised. As a result, the power-sharing Assembly and Executive were doomed to failure. Latent splits within the party surfaced in an explicit way, with party members openly voting against the party whip while other members were actively involved in bringing down the Executive in the Ulster Workers' Council strike in 1974.

With the collapse of the power-sharing Assembly and Executive, direct rule was restored and, although there were a number of political initiatives in the interim, self-government for NI did not become a realistic prospect until the GFA of 1998.

The principles which guided the UUP in the negotiations leading to the GFA can be found in the party's constitution. At its core is support for NI's continued position as an integral part of the UK. The party recognises the principle of self-determination for NI but only on the basis of mutual consent. Linked to this was the requirement of the revoking of Articles 2 and 3 of the constitution of the Republic of Ireland (which embodied the RoI's claims to sovereignty over NI) should an agreement be reached. Having secured the inclusion of these principles in the GFA, the UUP backed the agreement and the institutions, which would be established by it. In the intervening period between the signing of the Agreement and devolution day on 2 December 1999, all the political parties continued to formulate their interpretation of the GFA and in particular their party's stance on the sequencing of its key features. The core issue was whether or not there would be 'prior decommissioning', in other words, 'guns before government'.

All of the NI political parties were engaged in debate on this core issue but for the UUP and SF it became an issue which was to test and stretch party unity. While the SDLP and DUP were resolute in their respective total support or total opposition to the Agreement, the UUP and SF continued to debate at an internal party level as to how they should proceed.

The question of decommissioning, and the UUP's position on it, dominated intra-party relations in the period between the elections for the Assembly and the setting up of the institutions, and indeed continued for many months after this. To a greater degree than any of the other NI political parties, the issue threatened to cause the fragmentation of the UUP. The unique organisation of the UUP restricted the freedom of movement of the party's leadership. All key decisions and policy positions had to be approved by the party's Ulster Unionist Council (UUC), comprising over 800 members. The UUP leadership was constrained by the need to seek the approval of the UUC and was limited further by the evidence from the 1998 election that decommissioning could be a potential vote loser. Although the party went on to become the largest party in the Assembly, the party attained 21.3% share of the vote in the Assembly elections (a decline of 2.9% on the 1996 result of the election to the NI Forum), marking the party's worst ever performance in a NI election (www.ucl.ac.uk/constitution-unit/monrep/ni/ninov99.pdf, Nations and Regions, November 1999:31&32). Given that overall voter turnout had increased by 5.5% compared to 1996, the results suggested that some UUP voters had deserted the party. The UUP also secured its Assembly majority through the transfer of votes by Single Transferable Vote (4.6%), the system used for the elections. Clearly the UUP had gained from transfers from supporters of pro-agreement parties, most notably the SDLP. While the UUP's majority in the Assembly was undisputed, nevertheless its polling in the election served as a reality check on just how seriously issues like decommissioning were concerning UUP supporters.

The UUP continued to lose votes and in the 2003 election it was relegated to second position, as the DUP became the largest unionist party in the assembly. The electoral performance of the UUP in 2003 proved to be less dramatic than forecasters predicted. In fact, the UUP lost only one seat in the Assembly and increased its share of the vote from 21.3% to 22.67%, suggesting that it managed to retain most of its voters. More dramatic, and more worrying for the UUP, was the increase in the DUP's Assembly seats; it gained an extra ten seats. Two years later, in 2005, in elections to the Westminster parliament the party suffered badly in the polls with the number of parliamentary seats reduced to one (from six in the 2001 election) while the DUP increased its number of parliamentary seats by four (from five in the 2001 election).

54

In the elections to the restored Assembly in May 2007, the UUP received only 14.9% of the overall vote, gaining 18 Assembly seats and was relegated to third largest party in the Assembly.

The change in the UUP's electoral position since the Good Friday Agreement in 1998 can be seen in Table 9.

Table 9 *UUP Electoral Performance, Assembly and Westminster Elections 1998–2007)*

Assembly Elections	No of Seats	% share of the vote	Westminster Elections	No of Seats	% share of the vote
1998	28	21.25	2001	6	26.8
2003	27	22.7	2005	1	17.7
2007	18	14.9			

Following the routing of the UUP at the Westminster election in 2005, the party's leader, David Trimble (who had led the party into the talks and persuaded party stalwarts to accept the Good Friday Agreement and became First Minister of the new Northern Ireland Assembly), resigned. His replacement was Sir Reg Empey. The decline in support for the UUP continued at Assembly Elections in 2007, when the party gained only 18 seats with 14.9% of the vote.

What were the reasons for this decline? A central factor in the loss of electoral support for the UUP was divisions within the party. Party acceptance of the GFA had required careful persuasion by the party leaders, and their support was always tenuous. Decommissioning of IRA weapons proved to be the stumbling bloc on which the party would factionalise. The GFA had left the issue of decommissioning deliberately vague stating that:

> All participants accordingly affirm their commitment to the total disarmament of all paramilitary organisations. They also confirm their intention to continue to work constructively and in good faith with the Independent Commission and to use any influence they have, to achieve the decommissioning of all paramilitary arms within two years following endorsement in referendums North and South of the agreement and in the context of the implementation of the overall settlement."
>
> *(GFA, 20:3)*

The process of decommissioning would be monitored by the Independent International Monitoring Commission on Decommissioning but other than the general statement that decommissioning was to be achieved within two years, there was no clear schedule for it. The vagueness may have been necessary in order to get the deal done on Good Friday in 1998 but it cast a shadow over the new Assembly from the start.

For the UUP, decommissioning would be the ultimate litmus test demonstrating the extent to which SF had fully embraced and committed itself to the peace process.

Without any advance on decommissioning in the months after the Agreement, the party continued to be very suspicious and mistrustful of Sinn Féin and its commitment to the peace process, and also to the GFA and to the devolved institutions. The party suspected that SF was following a dual strategy of pursuing a political solution but keeping the military option open (www.ucl.ac.uk/constitution-unit/monrep/ni/ninov99.pdf, Nations and Regions, November 1999:34).

A breakthrough came in autumn 1999 when, under the leadership of George Mitchell, who had overseen the negotiations on the GFA, a review process was initiated. Mitchell was able to make progress with his proposal for the sequencing of decommissioning and the appointment to the decommissioning body of an interlocutor by all paramilitary groups. This compromise proved acceptable to both the UUP and SF, and the institutions of the GFA could be established. The UUP's leader, David Trimble, went to the Ulster Unionist Council to seek its approval for the new proposals. If these were accepted by the Council, devolution could at last take place.

The UUC's support was conditional; if decommissioning had not happened by January, then the UUP Ministers would resign their posts, forcing the collapse of the Executive. As devolved powers were transferred to NI on 2 December 1999, the Government of the Republic of Ireland amended Articles 2 and 3 of its constitution, rescinding Dublin's territorial claim to NI. A core UPP demand had therefore been met.

The power of the UUC was both the party's strength and its weakness. The need to have all key decisions and policy positions approved by Council meant that local party organisations could influence the leadership but it also constrained the leadership, as Trimble found, repeatedly forced to return to the Council for approval, with his power as leader diminishing each time.

The UUP entered the devolved institutions conditionally on assurance of substantive decommissioning by February 2000. A post-dated letter of resignation, effective from February, had persuaded the UUC to support Trimble's proposal to go into government with SF. However, the UUC's support was hardly overwhelming. A modest 58% of UCC members supported him, reflecting the pressure the leader was under from the party's rank and file. The next meeting of the UUC, scheduled for 12 February, served as a natural deadline for some movement on decommissioning, but this was shifted forward by the SoSNI, Peter Mandelson, to 31 January.

Although some progress appeared to have been made with the IRA announcement of an interlocutor, made one week after the Executive Committee had been established, the Unionist position solidified with Mandelson's acceptance of proposals for the reform of the RUC by the Patten Commission. The result was growing opposition within the UUP and further pressure on Trimble and the party leadership.

When the decommissioning body reported on 31 January 2000 that not only had there been no decommissioning but also no commitment to that effect, suspension of the Assembly was imminent and duly followed on 11 February 2000. The new NI Assembly and Executive Committee had operated for only ten weeks and two days.

Trimble's position continued to be further undermined by growing criticism of his policies from within the party and by the leadership challenge of the Rev Martin Smyth in March 2000. Trimble withstood the challenge but he hardly received a ringing endorsement from the party, garnering 57% of the UUC vote. While the UUC had voted to continue to support him as leader, the Council had nonetheless gone against the leadership by voting for a motion which meant that a return to government by the UUP would be conditional upon the retention of the name of the RUC. Trimble was becoming increasingly straitjacketed by his party. This was further underscored by the May 27 meeting of the UUC, when the support of his deputy, John Taylor, was not assured until the last moment and more vocal opposition came from Jeffrey Donaldson, Pauline Armitage, Derek Hussey, Peter Weir and Roy Beggs Jnr. The UUC continued to back Trimble but with a slim majority. The announcement by the IRA on 6 May 2000 that its weapons had been 'put beyond use' was sufficient, though barely, to enable the restoration of devolved powers on 29 May 2000.

The cloud of decommissioning hung over the restored Assembly and the UUP continued to lose support. In the general election of June 2001, the UUP lost four of its seats in Westminster. Clearly anti-agreement parties had gained at the expense of the UUP, and one of the prime beneficiaries was the DUP.

On 8 May 2001, Trimble had threatened to resign if there was no movement on decommissioning and he followed this through on 1 July 2001. In line with the GFA, which linked the roles of FM and DFM, new elections for these roles would have to take place within the Assembly. Some movement in relation to decommissioning came on 6 August 2001 when the interlocutor, General John de Chastelain, announced an IRA plan for "putting IRA arms completely and verifiably beyond use". The next day IRA issued a statement confirming the scheme. While the plan announced by General de Chastelain was a step forward, it only provided an indication of *how* but not *when* decommissioning would take place. A one-day suspension of the institutions on 11–12 August 2001 averted a full suspension but only postponed an all-out crisis, which developed in November with the elections for the FM and DFM. David Trimble was reinstated as First Minister, with a new Deputy First Minister, Mark Durkan (SDLP), who replaced Seamus Mallon. However, Trimble's election was only possible by the decisions of the APNI and NIWC to temporarily redesignate as 'Unionist' in the absence of sufficient support from his own party (www.ucl.ac.uk/constitution-unit/monrep/ni/ninov01.pdf, Nations and Regions: The Dynamics of Devolution, November 2001:3). Just before the elections of the FM and DFM, the first act of IRA decommissioning was reported, with two further acts following in April 2002 and October 2003.

By November 2002 NI was in crisis again. After recurring evidence that the IRA was still engaged in anti-democratic activities (three men had been arrested in Columbia in August 2001 and were suspected of providing aid to FARC rebels[1]; an intelligence raid had been carried out at Castlereagh police station in March 2002 and an alleged spy ring had been uncovered at Stormont in October 2002), the British PM, under pressure from the UUP, demanded "acts of completion" from the IRA. In essence, this was a call for full and verifiable disbandment of the IRA (www.ucl.ac.uk/constitution-unit/ monrep/ni/ni_february_2003.pdf, Nations and Regions: The Dynamics of Devolution, February 2003:4). The IRA's reluctance to do this resulted in the suspension of the Assembly in October 2002.

In the year that followed, the British and Irish governments worked to find a way out of deadlock and by October 2003 it seemed that the IRA was prepared to go some way to meet the demands. This was an important breakthrough, as one journalist commented: "there are not many conflicts in the world where one side renounces violence and scraps its weapons" (*Guardian*, 23 Oct 2003). A sequence of reciprocated announcements, planned for 21 October 2003, was designed to restore devolved government to NI. An initial announcement from the PM setting a date for new Assembly elections was to be followed by a statement by the interlocutor, General de Chastelain, on decommissioning. The final piece in the jigsaw was expected to be a statement of support from the UUP. Gerry Adams, speaking on behalf of SF and for the first time, overtly for the IRA, also made a declaration of "total and absolute commitment to exclusively democratic and peaceful means". However, de Chastelain's report that he had witnessed 'a considerably larger' act of decommissioning than any before, and Adams' statement on behalf of the IRA, were rejected by the UUP on the grounds that they lacked depth and transparency and so the plans for moving the process forward collapsed (*ibid*).

The UUP response to Adams' statement and de Chastelain's report was surprising as, in the build up to the announcements, the UUP seemed to be in agreement. The party's rejection served as a further indicator of the constraints that David Trimble was forced to work with in his party. In June 2003 he had faced another challenge to his leadership. Though he survived once more, the 46% vote for his challenger, Jeffrey Donaldson, showed the extent of division within the party. Subsequently the UUP MPs, Donaldson, Rev Martin Smyth and David Burnside, resigned the party whip at Westminster. This compounded Trimble's difficulties. When Trimble tried to expel the rebel MPs from the party, a judicial review overturned his actions (www.ucl.ac.uk/constitution-unit/ monrep/ni/ni_august_2003.pdf, Nations and Regions: The Dynamics of Devolution, August 2003:38).

Devolved government in NI forced a re-evaluation of core party principles and policies for all of the major parties. This was most profound within the UUP which had to find a middle way between safeguarding party principles and policies and accepting the politics of accommodation and adaptation. The difficulty this brought is evident in the internal wrangling within the party, played out in the public arena. These ongoing disputes and splits damaged the party, lost the party support and votes to the DUP and forced Trimble's resignation after the 2005 Westminster elections.

In October 2007 the UUP agreed to a series of reforms entitling all party members to vote in leadership elections and not just members of the UUC, thus opening the UUC to all members instead of selected delegates (*Irish Times*, 27th October 2007:8). The changes marked the beginning of the party's reform, with a clear attempt to: prevent any future stranglehold on the leadership by the UUC; to overcome the division and infighting that had surfaced in the aftermath of the GFA; and to reclaim voters lost to other parties and attract new ones to the reformed party.

Democratic Unionist Party

As the main anti-agreement unionist party, the DUP was resolute and vocal in its opposition to the GFA and the institutions established by it. Yet of all the Northern Ireland political parties, it is the DUP that has undergone the most radical shift in policy, from outright opposition, to a policy of wrecking the agreement from within, and then from 2007, to participating in government with Sinn Féin. Unlike the UUP, the DUP's Assembly representatives and party members have firmly supported the party's policy on the GFA and remained loyal to the party line. This unity in opposition to the GFA brought the party more support, largely at the expense of the UUP.

Participating in government with Sinn Féin marked a significant *volte face* for a party whose resistance to power-sharing was central to party policy. The party was established in 1971 by the Reverend Ian Paisley and Desmond Boal, largely in opposition to the policies of the liberal unionist PM, Terence O'Neill. Since its founding, the DUP has stood at the extreme right of unionism, refusing to counter any diminution of the union with Britain and actively opposing any threat to it. The acceptance of the GFA by all the other major political parties in NI presented a new challenge for the DUP: how to maintain its opposition to the GFA while at the same time preventing its own exclusion from the institutions of democratic government that the GFA envisaged.

In formulating its policies towards the GFA and devolved government, the DUP did not suffer from the internal dissension and factionalising of its UUP counterpart. Initially the DUP's position was not in dispute: no to the GFA; no to power-sharing with Sinn Féin.

In contesting the Assembly elections in June 1998, the DUP captured the votes of those in the unionist constituencies who opposed devolution in the context of power-sharing with 'unreconstructed terrorists'. It retained the vote of its traditional supporters but also made gains at the expense of pro-agreement parties, most notably the UUP. The party attained 20 seats in the new NI Assembly, representing 18.14% of the overall vote.

While refusing to work face to face with SF ministers in the Executive Committee, the DUP did nominate ministers to it, as it was entitled to do under the terms of the GFA. However, the DUP Ministers boycotted meetings of the Executive Committee as part of an ongoing strategy of undermining the Agreement from within.

This principled stance was compromised somewhat by the willingness of DUP Ministers and MLAs to work with pro-agreement parties, and most notably SF, in the Assembly and the Assembly committees. Some suspected that in refusing to participate in the Executive Committee, the DUP was playing both to its electorate and the media. But behind the scenes and out of view, DUP ministers and MLAs were actively engaged in the process of devolved government. This may have been simply *realpolitik*: the DUP knew that self-imposed exclusion would render it weaker and less effective in influencing the decisions of devolved government in NI. In a further sign that the party was prepared to accept the institutions established by the GFA, the DUP nominated a candidate for the position of Deputy Speaker of the Assembly in January 2000. In the event, its nominee, William Hay, was unsuccessful.[2]

The party's strategy followed the reasoning that while the NI Assembly existed, it would not exclude itself from it, but it would work to bring about its downfall. In the first phase of devolution the DUP continued to try to disrupt the Assembly. On 8 February 2000, the party made a third attempt to exclude Sinn Féin from office because of its refusal to commit to the principle of non-violence, which the DUP measured by full commitment to decommissioning. The party tabled a petition of concern in the Assembly, requiring 30 signatures for a cross-community vote to follow. This third attempt also failed (www.ucl.ac.uk/constitution-unit/monrep/ni/nifeb00.pdf, Leverhulme-funded Monitoring Programme Northern Ireland Report Number 2, February 2000:9).

When the suspended Assembly and Executive Committee were restored in May 2000 the DUP continued its strategy of disruption from within with a policy of rotating its ministers. The party continued to direct its attacks on SF. In May 2001 the DUP tabled a motion of no confidence in the SF Minister for Education, Martin McGuinness, but in the Assembly debate which followed, the motion failed.

This unwillingness to co-operate with SF was conducted in a public way in the Assembly chamber and through the media. However, behind the scenes, particularly at committee level the DUP engaged more fully than before in the processes of devolved government.

It became increasingly apparent that while the party continued to oppose the technicalities of the GFA institutions (sharing power with SF in the context of the Executive Committee), the DUP was proving itself capable of transcending the party's sectarian policies in the pursuit of cross-community interests and goals. The party's MLAs and Ministers appeared able to separate the two.

The DUP's stance appeared to have moderated. This indicated recognition that while most of their supporters continued to be concerned at the position of 'terrorists' in government, they nevertheless supported devolution and the benefits it could bring. This was reflected in a shift in party strategy – to one of seeking to recast the agreement rather than smash it.

Evidence of the success of this strategy came in the results of the Westminster elections in June 2001 when the DUP gained three seats bringing their total to five. In the constituencies of Strangford and East Londonderry, the DUP gained seats at the expense of the UUP. The DUP gained from disillusioned UUP voters and also because the party had moderated its stance on the GFA and its institutions, calling for the renegotiation of the GFA and for SF to honour its commitments.

The party recognised their electorate's underlying support for the concept of devolution and so tailored their electoral policies to match this. They also marketed party unity as a vote winner, contrasting themselves with the factionalising of the UUP in the months following devolution. Disunity meant weakness and the DUP gained strength from its unified approach.

Further evidence of the success of the DUP's strategy came in the November 2003 Assembly elections. The DUP increased its number of Assembly seats by ten (from 20 to 30), making it the largest party in the Assembly. The success of the DUP had been predicted but it was the scale of the success that was impressive. The DUP increased its share of the vote by over 7.5 percentage points (from 18.1% in 1998 to 25.6% in 2003). Equally impressive was the increase in the number of first preference votes secured by the party: from 146,989 in 1998 to 177,944 in 2003 – an increase of 30,955. Many of these first preference votes came from disaffected UUP voters but the DUP made significant gains at the expense of the smaller unionist parties such as the PUP and the UKUP. The changing electoral position of the DUP can be seen in Table 10.

Table 10 *Electoral Performance of the DUP 1998–2007*

Assembly Elections	No of Seats	Percentage share of the vote	Westminster Elections	No of Seats	Percentage share of the vote
1998	20	18.14%	2001	5	22.5%
2003	30	25.6%	2005	6	17.7%
2007	36	30.1%			

While the growing electoral success of the DUP was seen by many as a doomsday scenario, the gloom among pro-agreement supporters was tempered by the reassurances from the British and Irish governments that talks would continue to restore devolved government to NI. The DUP's bargaining position, fortified by its electoral success, would make that process more protracted but with the commitment to peace and devolved government still strong among the other pro-agreement parties, the DUP recognised that it would have to negotiate and compromise. The DUP's electoral hegemony gave it a powerful negotiating position and the party's leaders used this to try to force concessions. Ultimately, in the deal that restored devolved government to Northern Ireland – the St Andrews Agreement – a number of the UUP's demands were met, including a veto in a new devolved executive, a proposed cap on rates, reopening of local government reform and an opportunity to reverse the ending of academic selection (Wilford & Wilson, *Devolution Monitoring Programme – Northern Ireland*, January 2007:22).

One of the party's key objections to sharing government with Sinn Féin was its continued doubts about the IRA's position. When the Independent Monitoring Commission issued a report confirming that "the IRA had ceased all paramilitary activity and that the leadership no longer sanctioned any criminality" the DUP's position was harder to sustain (ibid:55). The DUP pressed for verification of this, and for a clear statement from Sinn Féin of its commitment to support policing and justice. When SF's Ard Fheis voted to support this, the DUP had to accept that the obstacles to sharing power with SF had been removed. The election that preceded the reconvening of the Assembly in May 2007, confirmed the DUP's and Sinn Féin's place as the dominant unionist and nationalist/republican parties in NI, enabling them to claim the offices of First Minister and Deputy First Minister respectively.

The DUP's decision to enter government with Sinn Féin seemed unimaginable to many and had been unattainable for so long. Why was it achieved in 2007? There are several reasons for this but it seems clear that the pressure from the British and Irish governments – that this was the last chance to reach agreement before a solution would be imposed – was an important factor. In any imposed solution, the DUP's power might be constrained. A degree of *realpolitik* underpinned the DUP's approach to power-sharing. With its electoral support at a peak, continued resistance to power-sharing could potentially become a vote loser, particularly in a climate when the popular will for a resolution was so strong.

Social Democratic and Labour Party

If the UUP was one of the victims of the changed political context in Northern Ireland after 1998, then the SDLP was the other. The party had played a central role in the peace process, and had been active in trying to end the conflict and bring about a solution for many years under the leadership of John Hume. In the 2007 Assembly elections the party gained 16 Assembly seats. Under the D'Hondt arrangements for allocation of ministerial posts based on party share of the vote, the party was entitled to only one ministerial post, taken by Margaret Ritchie at the Department of Social Development. This was in contrast to the Assembly and Executive formed in 1999 after the GFA, when in addition to the post of Deputy First Minister, the party held a further three ministerial posts and 24 Assembly seats.

The changed electoral fortunes of the SDLP was a result of the electoral rise of Sinn Féin. For more than thirty years the SDLP represented nationalist voters in NI who supported constitutional means for achieving political change. Since its founding in 1970, the SDLP was proactive in seeking a negotiated settlement for NI. The party's leader, John Hume, was often a lone voice, continuing to speak the constitutional message of non-violence when many others had given up. At times it was a very lonely and isolated position for Hume and his party to be in (Hennessy, 2000:19). The SDLP actively promoted the concept of inclusivity – for an agreement to work all parties had to be involved. Crucial to the GFA and the goal of devolved government was the inclusion of Sinn Féin in the political process, and a commitment to non-violence. The reward for the SDLP came with the GFA and the power-sharing institutions it established.

The origins of the SDLP lay in the Northern Ireland Civil Rights Association that had been formed in 1967 and many of the leaders of NICRA became influential members of the SDLP. The party became a channel for the representation of disaffected Catholic voters in NI, many of whom believed they had experienced discrimination (both political and socio-economic) first-hand under Unionist-controlled governments in Stormont. The SDLP has been an active participant in all political initiatives to secure peace in NI. SDLP ministers took seats in the short-lived power-sharing Assembly in 1974 but could do little to prevent its collapse under the pressure of the UWC strike. In the early 1990s Hume engaged in secret talks with SF to seek some way to bring about a resolution. In 1998 his efforts bore fruit with the signing of the GFA. In an era of great change the SDLP remained faithful to two basic and interlinked principles: the rights of all in Northern Ireland to the identity, ethos and way of life of their choice; and the pursuance of political and constitutional objectives by purely peaceful means (SDLP Manifesto, 1998).

The signing of the GFA and the setting up of the devolved institutions realised a cherished goal for the SDLP. In the years and months following the GFA, and especially during the periods when the Assembly was suspended, the SDLP had been active in trying to achieve progress on the issue of decommissioning – seeking to exert pressure on both Trimble and the UUP, SF and the British government at critical times.

In the June 1998 elections to the new Northern Ireland Assembly the SDLP attained 22% of the overall vote, representing 56% of the Nationalist vote (a slight increase on 1996 of 0.6%). It received 24 seats in the Assembly (22.2% share of total Assembly seats). The party made some gains through vote transfers. As the second largest party in the Assembly, the party was entitled to nominate a member to the position of DFM and Seamus Mallon was nominated to the role. As the issue of decommissioning began to dominate, the SDLP was careful to avoid alienating nationalist voters by open criticism of SF. However, as the impasse over decommissioning threatened to undermine the whole process, SDLP leaders sought to put pressure on SF and the IRA.

Increasingly, the reality for the SDLP was that as it pushed the peace process forward and integrated SF into democratically devolved government, the less secure its position as the leading nationalist party became. The need to keep the paramilitary wing on board and the strength of its electoral support meant that SF would dictate the pace of decommissioning and would also dictate its own terms. As SF and decommissioning became the lynchpin on which the whole GFA and devolved institutions would survive or fall, SF became increasingly aware of its powerful position. In contrast, the SDLP response was to try to push the process forward in order to achieve resolution through statements and interventions.

This may have been because the SDLP stood to lose so much. In electoral terms it was already losing. From 1981 onwards the SDLP was forced to seek its marginal voters from republicans. In 1998, as SF became the publicly and politically acceptable face of Irish republicanism, unaligned and floating nationalist voters tended to give their backing to them. In the 2001 Westminster elections the slow drift from SDLP to SF continued. Though the SDLP retained its three seats with 21% share of the vote, SF made gains, winning the seats of Fermanagh South Tyrone and West Tyrone to bring their seat total to four with 21.7% share of the vote. The SDLP was relegated to the position of fourth largest party, a development that was repeated in the local council elections. In the wake of the elections there were calls for Hume to resign and in the following annual party conference in November 2001, Hume and Mallon stood down as leader and deputy leader. Mark Durkan and Brid Rodgers were selected by party members as their replacements.

The change of regime within the SDLP was not enough to halt the drift in votes away from the SDLP. In the 2003 Assembly elections, the SDLP suffered great losses in comparison to the other major parties. The party lost six assembly seats and saw its share of the vote decline to 16.98%, a decrease of 4.98% in comparison to the 1998 poll. Worryingly, though not unexpectedly, the party lost 60,416 first preference votes (from 177,963 in 1998 to 117,547 in 2003). This can only partly be explained by a switch in first preference voting from traditional SDLP supporters (Sinn Féin increased its first preference votes by 19,900). It seems likely that apathy overtook many traditional SDLP voters – whether this was the consequence of perceived lack of choice or a measure of satisfaction with the existing SDLP party and policies.

The fulfilment of the party's long term goal of devolved government for NI left the party with a new challenge: to adapt to the new politics in NI and to the new generation of voters. For most of the years of conflict, the SDLP could rely on the loyalty of its electorate, but the resolution of the conflict and the emergence of SF has made the nationalist electorate more volatile. In these changing circumstances, the SDLP, like the other major political parties, needed to adapt and change. The resignation of the party's 'old guard' of Hume and Mallon was the first stage in this process. For some, the problems for the SDLP arose from the 'three Ms': too male, too middle class and too middle of the road (*Guardian*, 24 November 2003:11). The electoral fortunes of the SDLP continued to suffer in the Assembly elections of 2007. The SDLP's declining electoral support can be seen in Table 11.

It is not unusual for single purpose political parties to flounder once their goal has been achieved. For example, anti-communist parties and movements in the former Soviet Union and Eastern Europe effectively disappeared once communist regimes had been removed and were replaced by democratic institutions and a plurality of political parties. The SDLP has not been a single purpose party but the underpinning principle

Table 11 *SDLP Electoral Performance 1998–2007*

Assembly Elections	No of Seats	Percentage share of the vote	Westminster Elections	No of Seats	Percentage share of the vote
1998	24	21.97%	2001	3	21%
2003	18	17%	2005	3	17.5%
2007	16	15.2%			

that have guided the party – peaceful resolution of the NI conflict, inclusive economic and social policies and economic prosperity for all – are closer to achievement than ever before (SDLP website). The changed political circumstances in NI have forced the party not only to reform its leadership, but also to refocus its policy towards an all-Ireland perspective and to try to realign the party through greater links with the Republic of Ireland's Fianna Fáil party (bbc.co.uk, 29 November 2007).

Sinn Féin

Sinn Féin has been the key beneficiary of the new arrangements in Northern Ireland. Of all NI's political parties, Sinn Féin was the one with the most to lose but also the most to gain from the talks process and any resulting settlement. The strategy of the politicisation of the conflict, involvement in democratic procedures and decommissioning, saw SF move from being a pariah on the margins of the political framework to being an integral part of the whole process and a serious contender in NI politics. While this altered position is as dramatic as it is historic, it did not come about rapidly but rather in a staged, almost piecemeal way.

Just over 100 years since its founding in 1905, a Sinn Féin leader took the role of Deputy First Minister of the Northern Ireland Executive. The party had emerged in the early 20th century as part of the opposition to Home Rule, with the separatist intent of the new political party evident in its choice of name: Sinn Féin – Ourselves Alone. Sinn Féin made its first foray into electoral politics in Ireland after the Easter Rising of 1916 and achieved a remarkable popular endorsement in the 1918 general election. After the Irish Civil War (1921–23), and de Valera's formation of a new party in 1926 (Fianna Fáil) Sinn Féin was relegated to the periphery of politics in Ireland. In NI it rarely made an electoral impact.

Following the split in the IRA in 1970, the Provisional SF emerged and by the late 1970s the party was beginning to undergo a change in thinking. While its ultimate goal remained unchanged – British withdrawal from Ireland – the methods for achieving this were rethought. This was partially a result of the hunger strikes in 1981. The election of hunger striker, Bobby Sands, as MP for Fermanagh-South Tyrone in the Westminster elections, showed the potential electoral power of Sinn Féin's supporters.

This was confirmed in 1983 with the election of Gerry Adams as MP for West Belfast. While SF MPs refused in protest to take their seats in the House of Commons, electoral support for the party could not be disputed. During the second half of the 1980s and into the 1990s the party pursued a dual strategy of the 'armalite and the ballot box'. The armed struggle would be continued but SF would try to make gains politically as well. The political/electoral strategy appeared to be working well. In 1997 Martin McGuinness was elected as MP for Mid Ulster.

By the 1990s two important factors were influential in further developing SF's political thinking on a resolution of the conflict. Firstly, while the IRA campaign continued – with grave injuries and fatalities to both members of the security forces and civilians – there was a growing popular disillusionment with the futility of the campaign. The IRA had continued to keep Britain engaged in NI for 30 years with neither side any closer to achieving their goals. This is linked to the second factor: developments internationally and specifically the collapse of Communism in the USSR (1991) and the removal of the apartheid regime in South Africa. SF had placed itself on the left of the political spectrum, identifying itself strongly with the revolutionary ideas of Marxism Leninism. The collapse of Communism in the USSR had shown the ideology to be defunct and no longer relevant to the altered socio-economic structure of the Soviet Union in the 1980s. When the very state, which had embraced and epitomised Marxism Leninism collapsed, it became harder for SF to present itself as a party of the left, pursuing its revolutionary goal.

The impact of the ending of apartheid in South Africa is equally significant for the change in thinking in SF strategies. SF and Irish republicans had long identified with South Africa's blacks and their long struggle against the white supremacist regime. There had been frequent exchanges of peoples and papers between SF and the African National Congress. Yet by the 1990s even this conflict had been resolved peacefully. The apartheid regime agreed to free elections and Nelson Mandela was swept to power as South Africa's first black President. The developments in South Africa served as a reminder for SF and the IRA of how goals could be achieved by peaceful means. It was also a reminder that as other conflicts around the world were being resolved the conflict in Ireland continued to drag on with little real progress.

These factors help to explain the willingness of SF to engage in talks in the 1990s and to reach the point in 1994 when the IRA declared a ceasefire, making it possible for the party to enter talks on a settlement. The end result of the talks process, the GFA, was historic in many ways, not least because it provided the opportunity for SF to engage in government in NI for the first time in its history. SF had clearly undergone a change in strategy: from seeking to 'smash Stormont' it was now prepared to work in it.

In signing up to the GFA, SF, like the other political parties, had accepted the need for compromise. For SF this meant the inevitability of decommissioning. While the party accepted the reality of decommissioning, it played the politics of negotiation to great effect, acknowledging that while decommissioning would take place, it would be a process which it would control rather than the British government or the unionist parties. Decommissioning was the single key issue which undermined the early years of devolved government. A failure to decommission resulted in the suspension of the devolved institutions from February–May 2000 and two one-day suspensions in August and September 2001.

During the period between the signing of the GFA and actual decommissioning (which began in October 2001), the positions of the DUP and SF shifted. Both parties had entered the devolved institutions under different pretexts: for the DUP, it was to destroy the institutions from within and for SF, it was to use them as a springboard to working for a united Ireland. However, as the tangible benefits of the peace dividend were felt by all people in NI, both parties recognised the support among the electorate for devolved government for NI. Consequently, both SF and the DUP ceased to look beyond Stormont and the devolved institutions and began concentrating their efforts there.

Electorally, SF's position improved as the peace process developed. The growth in its support was clearly demonstrated in the elections to the NI Assembly in June 1998. SF attained 17.6% of the vote, an increase of 2.2% on the 1996 elections. The party gained 18 seats in the Assembly with 16.7% share of the seats. As the fourth largest party in the Assembly, SF had clearly gained political legitimacy. Entitled to nominate two ministers in the Executive Committee, SF nominated ministers to the two 'big spending' departments: Education and Health.

As SF became actively engaged in the politics of devolved government and in governing NI, its credibility and legitimacy increased and this translated into further electoral gains. In the June 2001 Westminster elections SF's share of the vote increased to 21.7%, holding its two existing seats and gaining another two. The SDLP was relegated to fourth largest party and SF exceeded the SDLP in terms of Westminster seats. At the local elections SF also made gains, taking 21% share of the vote and electing 108 councillors throughout NI.

The rise of SF continued in the 2003 elections with a reversal in positions held by the two nationalist parties. SF now became the largest nationalist party in the Assembly. The party increased its number of Assembly seats from 18 to 24. Its share of the vote increased from 17.6% in 1998 to 23.52% in 2003. The number of first preference votes for SF increased by 19,900 votes from 142,858 in 1998 to 162,758 in 2003. A number of factors help explain this, including a change in voting behaviour among the nationalist community, disillusionment with the SDLP among its traditional clientele and support for SF from a younger generation with less experience of IRA violence in their formative years. SF's image as a young, diverse and pro-active party also appealed, especially when placed alongside the more reactive SDLP, and this was certainly a contributing factor. For journalist Eamon Phoenix, the explanation lies with a generation of young and first time voters who have "no folk-memory, of the glory days of Hume, Mallon and the civil rights struggle, nor indeed of the thirty years of the Troubles." (*Irish News*, 2003)

Sinn Féin's popularity was underlined further in the elections to the 2007 elections when it secured 28 seats in the restored Assembly, gaining four ministerial posts, in addition to the post of Deputy First Minister. Sinn Féin's electoral performance is show in Table 12 below.

Table 12 *Sinn Féin's electoral performance 1998–2007*

Assembly Elections	No of Seats	Percentage share of the vote	Westminster Elections	No of Seats	Percentage share of the vote
1998	18	17.63%	2001	4	21.7%
2003	24	23.5%	2005	5	24.3%
2007	28	36.2%			

The politicisation of the conflict resulted in an improvement in SF's fortunes. Gaining electorally while adapting to the support of its electorate for the devolved institutions, SF, in the first Assembly, engaged in the business of governing NI. Members participated fully in the Executive Committee, in the Assembly Committees and in the Assembly itself. Perhaps more than any of the other parties in NI, the party proved itself to be the most adaptable; it recognised the need to engage in talks; accepted the compromise of the abolition of Articles 2 and 3 of the Republic's constitution, power-sharing with former opponents; and the ultimate test, decommissioning. The IRA's announcement that the war was over, its confirmation that decommissioning of weapons had taken placement and the support of SF's Ard Fheis in endorsing the leadership's policy of supporting the institutions of justice and policing in NI, made possible the restoration of devolved government in Northern Ireland in 2007. Sinn Féin was central to this.

Other political parties

After the 2007 election only ten of the 108 seats in the NI Assembly were taken by parties other than the ones discussed above – DUP, SF, UUP and SDLP. The Alliance Party took seven seats, two seats went to electoral candidates standing for the Independent Health Coalition and the Green Party respectively and one candidate stood as an Independent.

This minority position reflects the political landscape in NI where the dominant blocs are unionist and nationalist and the political centre is in reality very small. The main smaller party occupying the political centre has been the Alliance Party, whose number of electoral seats and share of the vote has remained small but fairly constant This is illustrated in Table 13.

One of the problems confronting smaller political parties in Northern Ireland i one that is common in most liberal-democratic systems, ie their minority status an

Table 13 *Electoral performance of NI's smaller political parties 1998–2007*

Assembly Elections	No of Seats	Percentage share of the vote	Westminster Elections	No of Seats	Percentage share of the vote
1998	6	6.5%	2001	0	3.6%
2003	6	3.7%	2005	0	3.9%
2007	7	5.2%			

Table 14 *Seats in NI Assembly held by MLAs from smaller political parties*

Political party	1998	2003	2007
Alliance	6	6	7
United Kingdom Unionist	5	1	
Progressive Unionist	2	1	
NI Women's Coalition	2	0	
Others	3	1	3
Total	18/108	9/108	10/108

political peripherality. It is this that renders them almost unelectable, with little prospect of being able to form or participate in government and therefore less attractive to the electorate. Their main function is to challenge the dominance of the major parties and to keep the concerns of their electorate on the political agenda. The unique structure of the NI Executive, based on the D'Hondt system, means that smaller political parties have no prospect of becoming 'kingmaker' parties – more typical of majoritarian, or first past the post electoral systems – in which major political parties need the support of small parties to form a government.

Smaller political parties in NI operate in a difficult context, forced to exist in a political environment dominated by the unionist and nationalist blocs and rendered ineffective in the Assembly chamber by the weighted voting procedures introduced by the GFA. In spite of these constraints, minor parties recognised their power in the first Assembly and its committees while pressuring for changes in voting procedures, which would directly benefit them.

In the first Assembly there were four smaller parties represented plus three independent unionists. In the 2003 elections this was reduced to three and one Independent candidate. By the 2007 election there were only three smaller parties represented in the Assembly: the Alliance party, the Progressive Unionist Party and the Green Party, with a further one MLA standing as an Independent candidate. The decline in the number of smaller parties represented in the Assembly reflects the sharp polarisation of politics in NI in the years after the GFA, with the position of the smaller parties increasingly squeezed.

In the three Assembly elections, turnout has remained fairly constant: 69.9% in 1998; 63.1% in 2003; and 62.8% in 2007. The higher voter turnout in 1998 may be linked to that election's function as a 'founding election', and people were more highly motivated to vote. The smaller parties may have gained from this. In the subsequent elections, their share of first preference votes was smaller. For example, the number of votes for the Alliance Party fell by more than half in the 2003 elections (25, 372), compared to their share of first preference votes in the 1998 election (52,636). The party's position recovered somewhat in the 2007 elections, winning 36,139 first preference votes, representing 5.2% of the overall vote (Wilford and Wilson, *Devolution Monitoring Programme – Northern Ireland,* April 2007: 68).

Of the smaller political parties in NI, the **Alliance Party** has the longest history. The party was founded in 1970 by liberal unionists who had supported the reforms of liberal unionist PM, Terence O'Neill. The Alliance Party attracted those from both sides of the community in Northern Ireland who found that their political interests were not being served by parties from either the unionist or nationalist blocs.

The Alliance Party presented itself as the party of the centre, but in NI the political centre is very narrow. Nevertheless, the party has managed to maintain this position in NI politics for more than thirty years, though it never managed to attain a seat in Westminster.

As a party of the centre, committed to inclusivity and constitutional politics, the APNI gave full party backing to the GFA. Its electorate endorsed this position with the party attaining 6.5% share of the overall vote in the Assembly election, entitling the party to six seats in the Assembly. This, however, was insufficient for the party to be entitled to nominate ministers to the NI Executive under the D'Hondt system (see Appendix 1) even though former leader, Lord Alderdice, was appointed speaker of the NI Assembly. When the Transitional Assembly was convened in 2006, Eileen Bell of the Alliance Party was appointed Speaker.

In the past the APNI never found itself in the favourable position of smaller parties in other political systems: that of being able to decide the fate of a parliament or government. This changed for the APNI when the party effectively became kingmaker in the securing of the Assembly's election of Trimble as FM and Mark Durkan as DFM in November 2001. The APNI temporarily redesignated three of its MLAs as unionists. The redesignation was something the party objected to but was prepared to tolerate if it would secure the future of the devolved institutions. However, the party used its powerful bargaining position to extract promises of a review of voting procedures, which could make the voters of minor parties count in key votes (*Belfast Telegraph,* 2001).

The critical role played by the APNI in securing the future of the devolved institutions brought the party a number of benefits, not least highlighting the political position of a party which in recent years had often been overshadowed by the main parties. It also highlighted the weaknesses of the GFA in its voting procedures of weighted majorities, which militated against parties not designated either unionist or nationalist. The APNI emerged from the crisis in a stronger position – with a raised profile in the Assembly and in the media and having extracted a guarantee of a review of voting procedures. In the St Andrews Agreement (2006) reforms to parties' redesignation sought to prevent a similar occurrence.

The APNI has managed to survive a volatile political climate in NI from 2003, as the more dominant parties jostled for position and voters. Other small political parties that had broken through in the 1998 election folded and eventually wound up their party operations. This was the case for the NIWC.

The formation of the **NIWC** in April 1996 marked a historic first for NI – the emergence of a specifically female political party. The party did not, however, set itself out to be a voice for radical feminism in NI. Rather, the formation of the NIWC was recognition that the interests of Northern Ireland women, usually interests that were more socio-economic rather than sectarian, were not being adequately represented by the existing political parties in NI. Though a minor party, the NIWC gained rapid approval from the electorate. In the 1996 election to the NI Forum, 70 women from across Northern Ireland's religious and class divide contested the elections on the principles of inclusion, accommodation, human rights and equity (NIWC, website). The party polled a 1.6% share of the vote in the Assembly elections in 1998. The NIWC was also a prime mover in the talks on a NI political settlement, and it is an indicator of the party's influence that the Civic Forum for Dialogue, one of the institutions set up by the GFA, was initially proposed by the NIWC (Wilson, *Agreeing to Disagree*, May 2001:79).

The party was truly cross-community and in the 1998 elections to the NI Assembly the party gained two Assembly seats: Monica McWilliams for South Belfast and Jane Morrice for North Down. In the first Assembly the NIWC was active in the parliamentary chamber and at committee level, championing socio-economic issues rather than sectarian politics.

The NIWC was unequivocal in its support for the GFA and devolved government. Like the APNI, the party acted in November 2001 to secure the devolved institutions by redesignating as unionist in order to get David Trimble elected as FM and Mark Durkan elected as DFM. However, the party did not find itself in the more powerful bargaining position of the APNI. With only two members, the redesignating of the NIWC was not enough to swing the crucial vote. This underlined the party's position in NI politics. Never strong enough to force change on its own, its presence however did ensure that wider issues, other than simply party politics, were kept on the agenda. In many respects the NIWC always had a threat hanging over it. In other political systems where coalition parties emerged during a transition of power or regime change, these coalition parties have tended to fade away once a stable political environment has been restored. A party such as the NIWC would have to work even harder to secure its own presence in the political framework once devolved government was consolidated. The other danger was its marginalisation by the more dominant blocs and this was the case in the 2003 election. The party lost both its Assembly seats and saw a decline in its first preference votes of 7,234 (from 13,019 in 1998 to 5,785 in 2003). The formation of the NIWC seemed to herald a new dawn in the traditional, male dominated, bipolar political environment of NI. With the party's elimination from the Assembly, that new dawn proved to be short lived. In 2005 the party's offices were closed and in 2006 the party was formally wound down (bbc.co.uk, 23 Feb 2006).

Other small parties that contested the 1998 election were the UK Unionist Party (UKUP) and the Progressive Unionist Party (PUP).

The **UKUP** was founded in 1995 by barrister, Bob McCartney, a former member of the UUP. Its aim was to represent those voters in NI who preferred NI to be viewed as an integral region of the UK. McCartney stood as the UKUP candidate for the constituency of North Down in 1997 and was elected MP. In the Assembly elections of June 1998 the party polled 36,541 votes, representing 4.5% share of the vote and gained five seats in the Assembly. The party's fortunes took a nosedive in the Westminster elections of 2001 when Bob McCartney lost his seat to the UUP candidate, Sylvia Hermon. The party's decline continued further in the 2003 elections as its Assembly presence was reduced to one seat and its share of first preference votes declined to 5,700.

The party was persistent in its opposition to the GFA. It refused to participate in the talks process and, while its members sat in the Assembly chamber, its position was largely obstructionist. The party's loss of support in the 2003 elections was due partly to internal divisions which resulted in former UKUP MLAs standing as candidates for the Northern Ireland Unionist party.[3] The realisation among anti-agreement voters that smaller parties such as the UKUP could do little to effect change on their own was another factor.

Despite its poor showing at the 2003 election, the party contested the 2007 election with party leader, Bob McCartney, standing in multi assembly seats on an anti St Andrews Agreement platform (bbc.co.uk, 9 March 2007). The party failed to gain any Assembly seats in the election.

In the 2007 Assembly elections the **Progressive Unionist Party** gained one Assembly seat, thus retaining its single seat position of 2003. In the 1998 Assembly elections the party had gained two seats, with 2.55% share of the vote. By 2003 this was reduced to 1.16% and in the 2007 elections the party's share of the vote was 0.6%. The party appears to be retaining only a small core of supporters, losing votes in successive elections.

Although founded in 1979, the PUP attained a high political profile only on entry to the NI Forum in 1996. The party was involved in the negotiations leading to the GFA and backed the GFA and the devolved institutions. It was committed to joint responsibility between nationalists and unionists as the best means of governing NI, underpinned by the principle of consent (PUP website). While active in the Assembly and its committees, the PUP, like the other minor political parties in NI found it difficult to break through the dominance of NI politics by the main unionist and nationalists blocs.

At Assembly level the party's influence was limited, though it had more success in the area of local politics. Associated with the UVF, the party championed the rights of the working class. Its strongholds are the loyalist areas of Belfast and it was from the constituency of East Belfast and North Belfast respectively that the party's first two MLAs, David Ervine and Billy Hutchinson, were elected in 1998, garnering 20,634 votes. Since the mainstay of the party's support comes from working class loyalist areas, it was unlikely to increase its electorate substantially. The challenge for the party was to maintain and retain its support. This required a strong emphasis on direct contact with MLAs and the development of a type of clientism. The difficulty for parties such as the PUP in the post GFA context was that while they were popular at local level, in the Assembly they were overshadowed by the large anti-agreement parties.

In the 2003 elections the party just managed to secure a presence in the Assembly, retaining one seat but seeing its share of the first preference vote decline by 12,602 to 8,032. In January 2007 the party's leader and founder, David Irvine, died suddenly adding to the misfortunes of a party that was already struggling electorally.

In what is perhaps a glimmer of hope that there is room for minority parties in Assembly, the **Green Party of Northern Ireland** won its first ever seat in the NI Assembly in the 2007 elections. Brian Wilson, the party's NI chairperson, was elected in the tenth count after polling 2,839 first preference votes (bbc.co.uk, 9 March 2007). Its electoral manifesto outlined the party's position:

"Green politics weave economic, social and environmental problem-solving together to tackle the roots and not just the symptoms of our ecological change" (Green Party Manifesto, 2007:2).

The success of the Green Party's candidate may reflect growing popular awareness of environmentalism at a time when the causes and possible solutions to climate change are hotly debated. As a cross community organisation, the Green Party has a growing constituency of supporters willing to give it their first preference votes, and a significant number of other voters who are willing to see their votes transferred to it.

Summary

The changing political context in Northern Ireland is in part the result of changes of strategy of the major political parties. This has been most profound in the case of the DUP, which has undergone a strategic shift in sharing power with Sinn Féin, and in the case of Sinn Féin, succeeding in bringing about an end to IRA activity, decommissioning and ultimately, recognition and acceptance of policing and justice in Northern Ireland. These strategic shifts have had a significant impact on the other political parties, drawing votes from the mainstream constitutional parties – UUP and

SDLP – so that the DUP and SF have become the dominant parties of Unionism and Nationalism, respectively.

Within the bipolarity that now characterises the political landscape in Northern Ireland, smaller political parties have struggled for survival. The Alliance Party continues to attract its traditional base of support, though not increasing it significantly, while parties like the NIWC have disappeared. However, the recent electoral breakthrough of the Green Party may be a signal that there is room for new and younger parties that do not have a history deeply rooted in the 'Troubles' but which address current and pressing issues of concern to all groups in NI.

Notes

[1] FARC: Revolutionary Armed Forces of Columbia

[2] William Hay eventually became Speaker of the NI Assembly in May 2007 – the first Speaker to be directly elected by the Assembly. www.niassembly.gov.uk/members/biogs_07/speaker.htm (accessed 1 May 2008)

[3] None of the NIUP candidates were elected.

Chapter 5
The Northern Ireland Electoral Systems

Several different electoral systems are used in Northern Ireland for electing political representatives. For elections to the NI Assembly, STV (Single Transferable Vote) is used. A PR system is used for local council elections. Members of the European Parliament are elected using STV. A majoritarian (first past the post) system is used for elections to the House of Commons at Westminster. The D'Hondt system is used for allocating party seats in Executive and Committee positions.

In this chapter you will learn about the:

- Northern Ireland Electoral Systems,

  and be able to

- assess the political impact of the different electoral systems in use in Northern Ireland

I N THE NEW STATE of Northern Ireland, established by the Government of Ireland Act 1920, MPs to the NI parliament were elected using Proportional Representation.

By 1929 this had been replaced by a majoritarian system – first past the post. This facilitated one party dominance, and with limited engagement by NI's nationalists in the NI parliament, the Ulster Unionist Party was effectively the party of government until the imposition of direct rule in 1972.

In subsequent attempts to bring about an end to the conflict in Northern Ireland and to restore self-government through a locally elected parliament, proportional voting systems were introduced to ensure both communities in NI would be equitably and fairly represented. While forms of PR are used for elections to the NI Assembly for elections to the European Parliament and for local elections, a majoritarian system – first past the post (FPTP) – is used for elections to the House of Commons at Westminster.

Electoral Systems in NI

		Proportional Representation	Majoritarian FPTP	Most recent elections
Local	Council	✓		2005
Regional (Devolved)	Assembly	✓		2007
Centre	Westminster*		✓	2005
Supranational	EU Parliament	✓		2004

Elections can be called at any time during the life of the parliament.

Voting in Northern Ireland

At the time of writing, the population of NI is 1,685,267 and there are currently 1,127,258 voters registered on the electoral register (Electoral Office, 2008:11). The eligibility criteria for electoral registration are age, citizenship and residency:

Age: aged 18 or over.

Citizenship: a British, Irish, Commonwealth citizen or a citizen of a member state of the European Union.

Residency: resident in Northern Ireland during the whole of the previous three-month period. Members of the armed forces and other public servants who are stationed overseas can register at their home address. British citizens resident abroad are eligible to register in the constituency where they last registered before they left the UK, provided this was not more than 15 years ago (Electoral Commission, 2006:2).

A number of measures have been taken to minimise the opportunity for electoral fraud. *The Electoral Fraud (Northern Ireland) Act 2002* brought about significant change to electoral law and practice in Northern Ireland, replacing the model of registration by household with a system of individual registration annually. The Act also required a specified form of photographic identification at polling stations before voters were issued with a ballot paper. These measures were designed to address the problems associated with electoral fraud and impersonation that had often accompanied elections in NI, captured with some underlying humour in a local catch phrase, 'vote early, vote often'. *The Northern Ireland (Miscellaneous Provisions) Act* became law on 25 July 2006, covering a broad range of areas including electoral administration and new provisions in respect of donations to political parties. The Act also introduced a donations control regime in Northern Ireland. From November 2007 political parties in Northern Ireland are required to provide the Electoral Commission with details of any donations they receive (Electoral Commission, 2008).

Parliamentary elections to House of Commons (Westminster) and the NI Assembly are based on the 18 Westminster constituencies.

Elections to the NI Assembly (PR-STV)

Elections to the NI Assembly are conducted using the PR-STV electoral system. This means that elections to the Assembly use a form of **proportional representation** known as **single transferable vote** (STV).

Proportional Representation is an electoral system designed to make sure that the candidates elected represent accurately the opinions of the voters, ie that the strength of each party in the elected forum is in proportion to its support among the people. The form of PR used in Northern Ireland is STV which is based on a quota system.

The core principles of the STV system were independently developed in the 19th century by Thomas Hare in Britain and Carl Andræ in Denmark. STV uses multi-member constituencies, and voters rank candidates in order of preference on the ballot paper in the same manner as under the Alternative Vote system. In most cases, this preference marking is optional, and voters are not required to rank-order all candidates – if they wish, they can mark only one (ACE Electoral Knowledge Network, 2008).

After the total number of first-preference votes is tallied, the count then begins by establishing the quota of votes required for the election of a single candidate. The quota used is normally the Droop quota, calculated by the simple formula:

$$\text{Quota} = (\text{votes} / (\text{seats} +1)) +1$$

The result is determined through a series of counts. At the first count, the total number of first-preference votes for each candidate is ascertained. Any candidate who has a number of first preferences greater than or equal to the quota is immediately elected.

In second and subsequent counts, the surplus votes of elected candidates (ie those votes above the quota) are redistributed according to the second preferences on the ballot papers (ACE, 2008). This is illustrated on page 78 by an example from the constituency of North Down in the 2007 Assembly elections.

Each voter has only one vote, but they can ask for it to be transferred from one candidate to another to make sure it is not wasted. This is done by numbering the candidates 1, 2, 3, 4, 5 and so on instead of just putting an **X** against one of them.

In elections to the NI Assembly, six MLAs are elected from each of the UK parliamentary constituencies. These are known as multi member constituencies.

This means that voters have a range of representatives to choose from and to transfer their vote to.

After the polling station has closed, the counting of results begins. Firstly the votes are sorted according to the first preferences of the voters. Each candidate is allocated every ballot paper on which there is a 1 against their name. It is at this point that invalid ballot papers are adjudicated, the total number of valid votes counted and the quota worked out. Any candidate who is then found to have reached the quota of votes is elected.

Some candidates may then have a surplus over the quota. Others may have so few votes that they can be eliminated from the contest. The remaining stages of the count

Results from the constituency of North Down, Assembly election, 2007

Candidate	Party	Status	Count	Votes	%
Alex Easton	DUP	**Elected**	1	4,946	16.1
Peter Weir	DUP	**Elected**	10	3,376	11.0
Stephen Farry	AP	**Elected**	7	3,131	10.2
Leslie Cree	UUP	**Elected**	10	2,937	9.6
Brian Wilson	GP	**Elected**	10	2,839	9.2
Alan McFarland	UUP	**Elected**	10	2,245	7.3
Alan Graham	DUP	Eliminated	10	2,147	7.0
Marion Smith	UUP	Eliminated	10	2,098	6.8
Robert McCartney	UKUP	Eliminated	7	1,806	5.9
Brian Rowan	IND	Eliminated	7	1,194	3.9
Alan Chambers	IND	Eliminated	8	1,129	3.7
Liam Logan	SDLP	Eliminated	9	1,115	3.6
James Leslie	Con	Eliminated	4	864	2.8
Deaglan Page	SF	Eliminated	3	390	1.3
Elaine Martin	PUP	Eliminated	3	367	1.2
Chris Carter	IND	Eliminated	2	123	0.4
Total valid vote				**30,707**	**53.4**
Turnout				**30,930**	**53.8**

Quota	4,387	Electorate	57,525

Notes on the Table

Source: news.bbc.co.uk/1/shared/vote2007/nielection/html/201.stm. Accessed 1 May 2008.

There were sixteen candidates contesting the election, thirteen presenting a range of political parties and three standing as independent candidates. Only one candidate met the quota in the first instance and he was elected. The other five candidates were elected through the transfer of votes.

are concerned with the transfer of surpluses or the elimination of candidates with the least number of votes.

When there are no more preferences expressed on a ballot paper it is retired from the count as 'non-transferable' and those ballot papers cease to have any further influence on the result (Electoral Commission, 2008).

PR is used for electing political representatives in a number of states. The particular form used in NI, STV, has also been used by the Republic of Ireland since 1921.[1]

There are a number of advantages associated with proportional systems of electoral representation. One of the most important is that PR ensures parliamentary or legislative seats are allocated in direct proportion to a party's share of the vote, unlike majoritarian systems where the party with the largest number of seats wins. PR means that a greater range of political views can be represented as the system is structured around multi member constituencies. In Northern Ireland, however, this can mean that there may be two or more candidates from the same party in each constituency, reflecting the dominant unionist and nationalist blocs. This means it can be difficult, though not impossible, for smaller parties to get elected, as votes are likely to be transferred between party members.

One of the criticisms of PR is that it can lead to coalition governments and a fragmented party system. In NI, PR has been designed specifically to lead to coalition where all political parties are represented, in proportion to their overall share of the vote. However, the presence of a range of political parties in a coalition government can impede decision-making, making it a lengthy and deliberative process in which all parties seek to exert their influence. Some of the risks associated with PR, for example the opportunities it can offer extremist parties to gain electoral seats, have not challenged the NI system, as parties tend to be situated within the two dominant blocs. At the 2007 election this was commented on by a local news correspondent who noted:

"It's best to think of the democratic process in Northern Ireland as consisting of two separate elections conducted in parallel, one within the Protestant community, and one within the Catholic." ('A tale of two polls', bbc.co.uk 9 March 2007)

Another criticism of PR forms of electoral systems is that they can be complex and difficult for voters to understand. In Northern Ireland voters have been used to PR systems for a number of years: for example, the elections to the European Parliament are based on PR. However the potential for voter confusion should not be underestimated, as exemplified by the elections held in Scotland in May 2007. Voters were asked to vote in two different polls on the same day using two different electoral systems: elections for the Scottish Parliament (using a combined system of first past the post and Additional Member System (AMS) and local elections using STV. This was the first time local elections were held using STV and in pre election publicity voters were given guidance on how to vote. On the day, however, many voters were confused, resulting in approximately 100,000 spoilt votes.

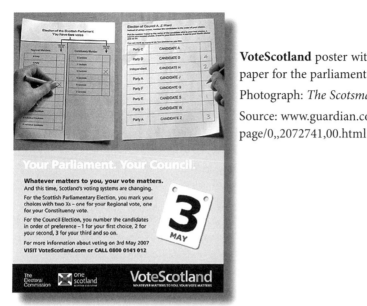

VoteScotland poster with a Scottish ballot paper for the parliamentary elections.

Photograph: *The Scotsman*

Source: www.guardian.co.uk/picture/page/0,,2072741,00.html

The STV system has a number of advantages. STV allows for choice between parties and between candidates within parties. Generally multi-member constituencies are relatively small so that a geographical link between voter and representative is retained. There is a danger however that when the electoral focus is on the individual politician rather than the political party, tensions can result within parties as effectively electoral candidates from the same party compete for votes, with the potential for encouraging 'clientelistic' politics (Electoral Knowledge Network, 2008)

Local Council Elections

Elections for local councillors for Northern Ireland's 26 local councils take place every four years using a PR electoral system.

Elections to the European Parliament

Elections to the European Parliament take place every five years. The PR-STV system is used to elect candidates. For these elections NI is treated as a region for which three MEPS can be elected. In the 2004 elections the MEPs elected were Jim Alister (DUP), Bairbre de Brún (SF) and Jim Nicholson (UUP). Turnout for the election was 51.2% (bbc.co.uk, 14 June 2004).

Westminster Elections – First Past the Post

The Northern Ireland electorate has always elected politicians to the House of Commons at Westminster. These elections usually take place approximately every 4–5 years and are based on a majoritarian, or first past the post system (FPTP). In this 'winner takes all' system, the person with the highest number of votes is elected.

There are a number of advantages associated with the FPTP system. It is relatively simple to use for the voter, requiring them only to express their preferred candidate by placing **X** against the candidate's name. FPTP tends to work most effectively in systems that are based on two party models, providing voters with a clear choice between two main parties. As it generally leads to single party government, it can result in strong and decisive leadership, especially where a party has been elected with a sizeable majority, as was the case with the Labour Party in Britain in 1997. It can also lead to strong opposition, where the defeated party can form a solid bloc.

However, there are a number of disadvantages associate with FPTP. A frequent criticism is that as it is 'winner takes all', those who did not vote for the winning party are effectively disenfranchised. In these circumstances the role of the party as parliamentary opposition and the legislative role in holding the government to account are important. Another criticism is that the system restricts the influence of smaller political parties, unless a political party forms a minority government, dependent on the votes of a smaller party enabling it to become 'kingmaker' (ACE, Electoral Knowledge Network, 2008).

The D'Hondt System

In Northern Ireland, an electoral allocation system know as the D'Hondt system is used to allocate ministerial positions and Chairs of Assembly Committees. Used widely across Europe, it is named after a 19th century Belgian lawyer (Victor D'Hondt) and is based on the 'highest average method'.

Based on the number of seats held by parties on the first day that the Assembly meets after the election, the D'Hondt system ensures proportional allocation of ministerial posts in the NI Assembly. The mathematical formula seeks to reflect the strength of a party's total support by taking into account its share of votes in relation to the number of seats already won. It means the average number of votes required to win one seat is almost the same for each party.

While the D'Hondt system is not normally used to form governments or administrations, the mechanism is used by Switzerland and Belgium to elect members to its federal bodies.

It uses a method of counting votes to ensure that each party receives a level of seats or ministerial posts, related to its level of popular support – but not at the expense of other parties which could lose out through other systems such as "first past the post" or proportional representation. The system differs from the single transferable vote (STV) in that it does not use a quota or formula to allocate seats or posts. Rather, these are allocated singularly and one after another.

A party's total vote is divided by a certain figure, which increases as it wins more seats. As that dividing figure increases, the party's total in succeeding rounds gets smaller. This allows parties with lower initial totals to win seats. In the first round of vote-counting, the dividing figure is one and therefore has no effect. However, the figure in subsequent rounds is the total number of seats gained plus one. Also under D'Hondt, the parties nominate committee chairs and committee members of the assembly. The parties can exclude themselves from the executive committee, and if it withdraws support from the committee its seats can be re-distributed under D'Hondt (bbc.co.uk, 29 November 1999).

This mechanism was thought ideal for the Northern Ireland Assembly because it ensures that the body works as a power-sharing institution. It was felt to be a suitable election mechanism for use in a divided society, aimed at ensuring cross-community representation (ACE, Electoral Knowledge Network2008). In the 2007 Assembly elections, the DUP, as the largest party had the first choice of ministry, followed by Sinn Féin, the second largest party, and so on.

Summary

Although the electoral systems in Northern Ireland may seem complex, particularly as different methods are used for different elections, nevertheless they have proved effective in achieving political representation in a generally fair and equitable way, based on parties' share of the vote. Though a majoritarian system is used for elections to the House of Commons at Westminster, the domination of politics in NI by one political party – in effect, the one party government that characterised politics in NI from 1921–1972 – is no longer possible under the current arrangements for elections.

Though smaller political parties have struggled to survive under the hegemony of the more dominant political parties from the Nationalist and Unionist blocs, the survival of the Alliance Party and the electoral breakthrough of the Green Party in the 2007 Assembly elections are signs that the NI polity continues to develop as a democratic state.

Notes

[1] Other states that use or have used PR-STV are Malta (since 1947), and Estonia (in 1990), (ACE, Electoral Knowledge Network 2008).

Chapter 6
Devolution in Practice

This chapter looks at how devolution has been implemented in NI. As well as evaluating how it has worked from 1999–2002 and from restoration in 2007, the chapter also looks at the other institutions that were set up as part of the GFA, and their role in underpinning the 'new democracy' in Northern Ireland.

By the end of the chapter you will be able to:

- provide an overview of devolved government in Northern Ireland
- explain the purpose and role of the North South Ministerial Council and the British Irish Council
- discuss the contribution of independent bodies such as the Civic Forum and the Human Rights Commission in supporting democracy and democratic institutions in NI.

O NE OF THE MOST encouraging developments in Northern Ireland's recent history has been that *when devolution works, it works well.* Unfortunately, in the ten years since the Good Friday Agreement was signed, the periods of time when Northern Ireland has been governed by direct rule have been longer than the periods of devolved government. The first Northern Ireland Assembly and Executive were overshadowed from the outset by the issue of decommissioning, and related to this, ongoing paramilitary activity, which fuelled mistrust. In spite of this, much was achieved during the tenure of the first NI Assembly and Executive, including 36 legislative Acts relating directly to Northern Ireland affairs (HMSO online, 2008). There was a very strong sense that the people of Northern Ireland were making decisions for themselves, reducing the democratic deficit that had existed for so many years.

However, some of the decisions taken, especially by Ministers, such as the decision by the Minister of Education (Martin McGuinness) to abolish the Eleven Plus selection examination for schools, divided rather than united popular opinion. In the St Andrews Agreement (2006), which ultimately made the restoration of devolved government possible, changes were made to the Ministerial Code to prevent so called 'solo runs' by Ministers, ie using their executive authority to take unilateral decisions, without reference to either the Assembly or the Executive Committee (Wilford & Wilson, January 2008:74).

When the Assembly was restored in 2007 procedures and structures were in place to enable it to get down to business quickly. This was due to the arrangements for a Transitional Assembly that had been put in place by the St Andrews Agreement. The purpose of the Transitional Assembly was to make it ready for the restoration of devolved powers and government. A speaker for the Transitional Assembly was appointed – Eileen Bell from the Alliance Party. The Transitional Assembly existed from 22 November 2006 until 30 January 2007 (NI Assembly, 2008), when, in line with the St Andrews Agreement it was dissolved, in advance of the elections that would precede the restoration of devolved powers.

However, despite the existence of mechanisms to facilitate a smooth transition from direct rule to devolved power – from the NIO to the NI Assembly – the capacity for the Assembly to influence policy and political life in Northern Ireland in the months after the restoration of devolved power was limited. This was due in part to the need to await a legislative programme encompassed in a Programme for Government that was not finally agreed until January 2008. In the interim, plenary sessions of the Assembly tended to focus on private members' business (Wilford and Wilson, January 2008:26).

When the proposed legislative programme was finally published (consisting of 18 bills, three of which were already under consideration), it was seen as 'unimaginative', reflecting the 'parity principle' of applying legislation agreed at Westminster to Northern Ireland rather than forging ahead with a new legislative programme directly linked to political and socio-economic needs of Northern Ireland (Wilson and Wilford, January 2008:10).

The fragile nature of the restored Assembly and the even more fragile Executive Committee, described by some as an 'involuntary coalition', meant that both the Assembly and the Executive Committee were unlikely to make any radical moves in the early days of re-devolution, at the risk of destabilising the status quo. This meant however that the actions of the Assembly and the Executive soon came to be seen as rather superficial and to some extent ineffectual. This was captured by the Chair of the Committee for the OFMDFM when he observed that the Assembly 'remains at the level of a school debating society, dealing with private members motions rather than real business' (Wilford and Wilson, January 2008: 26). While the outward face projected by the First Minister and Deputy First Minister was one of good humoured *bon amie*, below the surface cracks were already emerging. This became most apparent in emerging tensions between Assembly Committees and Executive Ministers and a cloud of political sleaze that began to drift across NI politics in early 2008.

The most public dissension between a Minister and an Assembly Committee occurred between the Minister for Education, Catriona Ruane (SF) and the Assembly's

Education Committee, chaired by Sammy Wilson, (DUP). The Minister had attended a meeting of the Assembly's Education Committee in January 2008 to discuss proposed changes to the eleven plus examination. Already a hot political potato, the Minister did little to either alleviate tensions nor appease the Committee's concerns, by an approach that appeared high-handed, disregarding the Committee's primary function, in scrutinising proposed legislation emanating from Executive departments.

This was far removed from the first meeting of the Committee in May 2007, attended by the Minister, when the Committee Chair outlined the function of the Committee stating:

"The Committee will have a scrutiny, policy development and consultation role, which will be vital in advising the Minister on the policy and plans of the Department" (NI Assembly: 2007).

The tense relationship between the Minister and the Assembly Committee highlighted the challenges facing NI's politicians as they struggle to reconcile party political interests with representative and ministerial responsibilities. In the heated exchange between the Minister of Education and the Chair of the Education Committee, this was articulated by the Minister saying to the Chair "I am unsure when you are representing the committee and when you are speaking for yourself." (bbc.co.uk, 2008).

In many respects it is in the Committees that the real business of the Assembly takes place, with Committees initiating or scrutinising legislation and co-operating on a cross party basis. While some meetings of Assembly Committees are open to the public and can be televised, often it is only when controversy occurs that they attract media and popular attention. Out of the public eye they engage in the tasks assigned to them by the GFA, with commentators noting:

"If there are nests of consensus within the Assembly they are to be found largely within the committee rooms" (Wilford and Wilson, January 2008:30).

During the period of the first Assembly, established after the Good Friday Agreement, the work of the Committees became increasingly demanding and burdensome for MLAs, leading to calls for reform of the Committee System. Following the restoration of devolved government in May 2007, a Standing Committee on Procedures was established. One of its first tasks was to undertake an inquiry into Committee systems and Structures which would:

- examine the membership of committees with particular reference to the number of members sitting on committees and the number of members serving on multiple committees;
- assess the use of substitutes in committees;
- examine the arrangements for quorums in committees;
- consider the possibility of the use of rapporteurs in committees;
- give consideration to the days and times on which committees should meet, the frequency of meetings and facilities for meetings;

- consider the procedures for voting in committees;
- assess the possibility of introducing Standing Orders to allow for joint committees;
- report to the Assembly, making recommendations on the findings of the Committee on Procedures into committee systems and structures (NI Assembly: 2008).

Reforms of the Committee system may enable the NI Assembly to become a more effective 'committee-led legislature', where the core business of the Assembly takes place at Committee level.

The committee system in comparative perspective

Some political scientists argue that given the complexity of many modern issues, a powerful Assembly needs a well developed committee structure if it is to exert real influence. Former US President Woodrow Wilson highlighted the importance of the US Committee system when he said "Congress in its committee rooms is Congress at work". The remit and work of committees can also be a measure of the effectiveness of a legislature, as the political scientist, Kashyap observed 'A legislature is known by the committees it keeps' (Kashyap in Hague *et al*, 1998:187).

Assemblies or legislatures can be classified into two types:

(i) talking assemblies, such as the British House of Commons, where floor debate is the real activity – the main issues are addressed in the Chamber;

(ii) working assemblies, such as the US Congress, where the core activity takes place in committees where legislators shape bills, authorise expenditure and scrutinise the executive. The NI Assembly could be described as a 'working assembly'.

An unexpected difficulty for the new NI Assembly and the Executive in 2007 and 2008 was the impact of investigations into the conduct of politicians elsewhere in the UK. The focus of such investigations was donations to political parties. Initially this had concentrated on donations to the political parties such as the Labour Party in England but soon spread to the Labour Party in Scotland. Northern Ireland did not escape the spotlight with journalists starting to look into the expenses of MLAs, employment by MLAs of family members and lobbying by Ministers in support of particular causes. The first casualty in relation to this in NI was to be a Junior Minister in the Office of First Minister and Deputy First Minister, Ian Paisley Jnr, who was forced to step down from office in February 2008 due to criticisms of links to property developers and questions about his assembly expenses (*Belfast Telegraph*, 26 February 2008).

This was a significant development in Northern Ireland affairs for two reasons. Firstly, it exposed the extent to which political life in Northern Ireland was grounded in a particularly local approach to politics that risked "giving rein to an old, clientelist politics" (Wilson and Wilford, January 2008:21). Secondly, and perhaps more significantly, it highlighted the extent to which the NI Assembly and its politicians were not isolated from concerns about public life and political conduct elsewhere in the UK. For example, investigations into MPs' expenses at Westminster were soon followed in NI to investigations by journalists in NI into MLAs' expenses. As issues of transparency, accountability and public scrutiny are discussed and debated in the UK media, similar debates take place in Northern Ireland. A case may have been made for NI's immature political development, particularly in the first phase of devolution (1999–2002), but by 2007–08, the media and voters were less sympathetic and less tolerant.

While the Assembly and the Executive constitute the key pillars of the democratic institutions in Northern Ireland, the other components of devolved structures, as outlined in the Good Friday Agreement, are the North South Ministerial Council (Strand 2), the British Irish Council (Strand 3), the Human Rights Commission, a Victims Commission, and a Civic Forum. These aspects of the Good Friday Agreement and arrangements for devolved government are considered in the following section.

One of the challenges confronting the architects of the GFA was to design mechanisms that would facilitate links with the Republic of Ireland and the UK in a way that was satisfactory to all constituencies. The North South Ministerial Council and the British Irish Council became the organisational and operational channels for these North-South and East-West relationships.

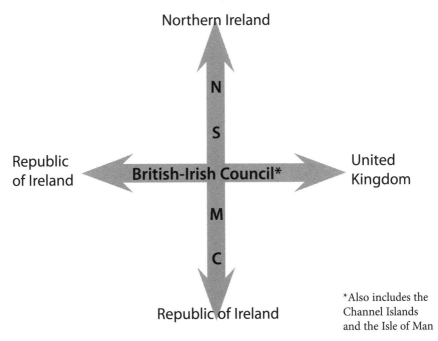

*Also includes the Channel Islands and the Isle of Man

The North South Ministerial Council

The main function of the NSMC is:

"... to bring together those with executive responsibilities in Northern Ireland and the Irish government, in order to develop consultation, co-operation and action within the island of Ireland..." (GFA, 1998, Strand 2:1).

It was intended that this should include implementation on an all-island and cross border basis on matters of mutual interest within the competence of the Administrations, North and South (*ibid*).

Representatives from both governments attend the NSMC. The NI representative are the FM, DFM and other relevant ministers, and the Irish government is represented by the Taoiseach and relevant ministers (GFA, 1998, Strand 2:2). Both sides are accountable to their respective legislative chambers: that is, the NI Assembly and the Oireachtas (*ibid*).

The NSMC meets in plenary format (ie, all members) twice a year, with the FM, DFM and the Taoiseach and government ministers from both administrations in attendance. The NSMC meets more frequently in sectoral format (eg agriculture, or health), with the ministers of the relevant sector or department attending. The council can also meet to deal with institutional or cross-sectoral issues and to resolve disagreement. The agenda for all meetings of the NSMC, whether in plenary or sectoral format, is agreed by both administrations in advance (GFA, 1998, Strand 2:3&4).

The remit for the NSMC, as specified in the GFA, is to:

- exchange information, discuss, consult and co-operate on matters of mutual interest;
- reach agreement on common policies in areas where there is a mutual cross border and all island benefit;
- to take decisions by agreement on policies for implementation in separate jurisdictions.

The NSMC was formally established on devolution day (2 December 1999) along with the other devolved institutions (the Assembly, Executive Committee and the BIC). The first plenary session of the NSMC took place on 13 December 1999 in Armagh. It was a historic occasion, with the Taoiseach and the President of Ireland, Mary McAleese, arriving together for the inaugural session. Since the inaugural meeting there have been five further meetings of the NSMC in plenary format – three before the suspension of devolved government (Dublin, September 2000; Dublin, November 2001 and Armagh, June 2002) and two since its restoration (Armagh, July 2007 and Dundalk February 2008) (NI Executive, 2008).

At its inaugural meeting, participants agreed six 'Areas of Cooperation'. These include Agriculture, Education, Environment, Health, Tourism and Transport. To implement joint policy six 'Implementation Bodies' operate on an all-island basis. The Implementation Bodies are:

- Waterways Ireland;
- Food Safety Promotion Body;
- Trade and Business Development Body;
- Special European Union Programmes Body;
- Language Body;
- Foyle, Carlingford and Irish Lights Commission (NSMC, 2008).

While the NSMC was designed to be a bridge between north and south, the actual work of the Council was impeded in its early years. This was due firstly to the periodic suspensions of the devolved institutions in the period 1999–2002; the boycott of the NSMC by DUP Ministers and the ban imposed by the FM in October 2000 on SF ministers attending NSMC sectoral meetings in response to the slow pace of decommissioning. SF contested the legality of the ban and its case was upheld in a judgement handed down by the Belfast High Court, in January 2001, which declared the ban illegal.

In putting in place measures to restore devolved government in Northern Ireland, the architects of the St Andrews Agreement (2006) sought to prevent any future boycott of devolved institutions through the revisions to the Ministerial Code of Conduct, requiring Ministers to agree to participate in devolved institutions as part of the Ministerial Pledge of Office (see chapter 2).

During periods of suspension, the work of other components of devolved government were also suspended. Essentially the work of the NSMC was 'frozen' though its secretariat continued to operate on a 'care and maintenance principle'. The cordial and productive relationship that had developed between Ministers and civil servants from the North and the South contributed to a climate of collaboration that was sustained, even during suspension and made the resumption of relations in the context of the NSMC less problematic once devolved power was restored. A degree of *realpolitik* appears to underpin this, with awareness that North-South cooperation is mutually beneficial. Developments that would have been unimaginable and indeed almost impossible just a few years earlier, such as the decision in 2007 by the RoI's national air carrier, Aer Lingus, to relocate to Belfast (from Shannon, in the West of Ireland) are indicators of this, as well as initiatives relating to transport (for example, the development of an hourly train service between Dublin and Belfast) and education (for example, a joint booklet on diversity aimed at primary school children) (Wilford and Wilson, January 2008:48; RTE News, 14 September 2007).

The British-Irish Council

The NSMC was designed to maintain and develop the relationship with the Republic of Ireland, and relations with the other constituent parts of the UK were to be channelled through the **British Irish Council**. While specific to Northern Ireland, the GFA was an integral part of the plan for devolved government in the UK which was an essential element of the programme of radical constitutional reform embraced by the Labour government under Tony Blair in its first term in office (1997–2001).

A core element of New Labour's policy was the devolution of power away from the centre (Westminster) to the regions of the UK. Thus, devolution in NI did not take place in isolation but was part of a wider plan for constitutional reform, which saw devolved government granted almost simultaneously to regional governments in Scotland and Wales. Devolution for NI came some months later than its Scottish and Welsh counterparts but by the end of 1999 all three regions within the United Kingdom were undertaking substantial aspects of government for themselves in newly elected legislatures and through new elected representatives (MLAs in NI, MSPs in Scotland and MWAs in Wales).

Consequently, while the GFA appeared to solve the problem of power-sharing in NI, the newly devolved and decentralised structure of UK government meant that NI was part of a wider trend of devolution. Seen in this context, devolution for NI represented an opportunity for NI to become an equitable partner in UK affairs, actively liaising and interacting with regional neighbours on issues of mutual concern and interest. The mechanism to achieve this would be the British Irish Council (BIC), or the Council of the Isles.

Strand 3 of the GFA foresaw the creation of a BIC, which would promote "the harmonious and mutually beneficial development of the totality of the relationships among the peoples of these islands" (GFA, 1998: Strand 3:1). For some, the BIC was the counterpart to the NSMC. It was viewed as a mechanism by which Unionist fears about the diminution of the union would be allayed – the BIC would strengthen, rather than weaken the union with Britain. Rather than viewing the GFA as the severance of the link with GB, Unionists saw it as a channel for building on the existing union in the new context of regional governments and it was presented to their electorate as such.

The BIC consists of representatives from the governments of the United Kingdom, Ireland, the devolved institutions in Northern Ireland, Scotland and Wales and the Isle of Man, Jersey and Guernsey. According to the GFA the main function of the BIC is to "exchange information, discuss, consult and use best endeavours to reach agreement on co-operation on matters of mutual interests within the competence of the relevant institutions" (GFA, 1998, Strand 3:5). Agreements between the member governments of the BIC are to be on the basis of consensus. Members will agree on common policies though member governments can opt out of participating on common policies and common action (GFA, 1998, Strand 3:7).

The BIC came into being soon after devolution day in December 1999 and the inaugural summit was held on 17 December 1999 in London. The summit was chaired by the British PM, Tony Blair. The BIC meets at summit-level at least once a year, more frequently at Ministerial-level and regularly at official level across its nine current work sectors (BIC: 2008).

The Council's work programme covers the following areas of mutual interest:

- misuse of drugs;
- the environment;
- the knowledge economy;
- social inclusion;
- health;
- tourism;
- transport;
- minority and lesser-used languages.   (BIC, 2008)

In its early years the low profile and relative inactivity of the BIC caused some observers to conclude that the BIC was in the doldrums ('Nations and Regions', August 2001). However, during the period of prolonged suspension the BIC continued to meet and facilitate collaboration and cooperation between and across UK region. Since it was established in 1999, the BIC has met ten times at summit level, and held almost 200 meetings or seminars at official and expert-level in all priority areas (BIC, 2008). The types of activities that members of the BIC have been involved with are developing networks allowing them to exchange views and share best practice. The BIC also notes that its members have, where appropriate, agreed practical co-operation on areas as diverse as the misuse of drugs; environmental issues; indigenous, minority and lesser-used language; social inclusion; and knowledge economy issues (BIC, 2008).

Developments in the UK since 1999, particularly the consolidation of devolved government in Scotland and Wales have given the BIC an added impetus, reflecting the foresight of the then NI DFM, Seamus Mallon, at the inaugural meeting of the BIC in 1999 when he observed:

"We have learned from Europe. It has been inspirational in the context of political developments. Not only do unique arrangements exist between such states as in Benelux or in the Nordic Council, but also regions have emerged from the shadow of nation states onto the international stage.

The BIC offers a new stage, a common platform for decentralised governments to meet the two sovereign governments. This council should enhance our democratic culture, not diminish it." (OFMDFM, 1999).

Cooperation with regional neighbours has been an important aspect of the work of the NI Executive since the restoration of devolved government, benefiting from their more extended experience of administration and government. One outcome of this has been a growing *rapprochement* between the new SNP administration in Scotland

91

and new administration in Northern Ireland. The first visit of Scotland's new First Minister, Alex Salmond, after the SNP victory in the Scottish elections in May 2007, was to Stormont. This is based on more than simply good will, reflecting a drive by Scotland's nationalist government to shore up devolution and extract greater powers from Westminster, especially tax raising powers. During his visit to the NI Assembly, Scotland's First Minister spoke about the possibility of a 'trio' of parliaments (Scotland, Wales and Northern Ireland) agreeing formal structures and a shared agenda, including further regional flexibility, possibly to cut Corporation Tax. The model for this, he proposed is the close relationships between Scandinavian countries (*Belfast Telegraph*, 19 June 2007). This was followed by a meeting in Edinburgh attended by NI's FM and DFM in February 2008 where talks focused on issues of mutual interest and concern relating to transport and renewable energy (NI Executive, 2008).

Another component of Strand 3 of the Good Friday Agreement was the establishment of a **British-Irish Intergovernmental Conference**. The BIIC subsumes the AIA of 1985. Essentially the BIIC represents the bilateral relationship between GB and RoI. Its purpose is to "promote bilateral co-operation at all levels on all matters of mutual interests within the competence of both governments" (GFA, Strand 3: BIIC:1 & 2).

The inaugural meeting of the BIIC was held on the same day as the BIC, 17 December 1999, and was attended by the British PM, the Taoiseach and representatives from the NI Executive. At the inaugural meeting, a list of topics of mutual interest and concern was agreed which included: asylum and immigration, EU and international issues, social security and fraud detection, education, misuse of drugs, organised crime and fiscal issues. A number of excepted and reserved matters were also identified: rights, policing, criminal justice, normalisation of security, cross border security co-operation, victims of violence, prison issues, drugs and drug trafficking and broadcasting (Devolution Monitoring, February 2000:24) Since the inaugural meeting the BIIC has enabled collaboration between the British and Irish governments at a bilateral level. A review of the BIIC in early 2003 found that the current machinery of the BIIC was working well and did not require significant change (BIIC, Joint Communiqué, 2 July 200). The last meeting of the BIIC took place in Dundalk in February 2007 (BIIC, 2007).

The GFA established institutions which would accommodate and reconcile political differences and enable NI to have a fully functioning government and assembly for the first time in more than 25 years. However, the framers of the Agreement also recognised that institutional changes alone would not be sufficient to bring peace, order and normality to NI. To achieve these, the framers established what could be described as secondary support mechanisms to strengthen the GFA and the new institutions. These support mechanisms consisted of:

- The Civic Forum;
- The Northern Ireland Human Rights Commission;
- The Equality Commission;
- Reforms in Policing and Justice.

The Civic Forum

The GFA provided for the establishment of a 'consultative Civic Forum' (GFA 1998, Strand 1:34). It was to be made up of representatives of the business, trade union and voluntary sectors, and other sectors agreed by the FM and DFM, and was to be a consultative mechanism on social, economic and cultural issues (*ibid*).

The inclusion of a Civic Forum in the final agreement was due to the efforts of the NIWC and its leader, Monica McWilliams. The creation of the Civic Forum recognised the fact that for there to be resolution and reconciliation, NI had to move beyond the politics of sectarianism towards the politics of accommodation and tolerance. In essence, this would mark the emergence of 'civil society' in NI.

The Forum held its first meeting in October 2000. Its 60 members had been nominated by various organisations in NI and by the FM and the DFM. Members were nominated from the following sectors: businesses; agriculture and fisheries; trade unions; voluntary and community groups; churches; culture, arts and sport; victims; community relations and education. Businessman Chris Gibson was appointed as its chairman (BBC Northern Ireland, Civic Forum, 6 October 2000).

The Civic Forum met regularly from its inception, providing a forum for discussing issues of concern in NI. However, it was unable to fully assert itself against a group of strong detractors both within and outside the Assembly. It was described as a "Fisher-Price parliament for the lap dogs and do gooders" and viewed as a cosmetic exercise, which was both powerless and pointless (Hearts and Minds, BBC Northern Ireland Oct 2000).

The Civic Forum did exert some influence on the work of the Assembly – responding to the Draft Programme for Government with some of its proposals incorporated into the final version.

However, when devolution was suspended in 2002, the Civic Forum was also suspended. It was not re-established when devolved power was restored in 2007. By 2008 when MLAs began to question the Executive about the Civic Forum, the DFM announced that any decisions regarding the Civic Forum would have to await the report from a review currently under way (NI Assembly Official Report, 18 February 2008).

Human Rights Commission

The establishment of a Human Rights Commission for Northern Ireland was an important component of the GFA (GFA, 1998: p17). The Commission was set up as an independent, statutory body in 1999. Its role is to promote awareness of the importance of human rights in Northern Ireland, to review existing law and practice and to advise government on what steps need to be taken to fully protect human rights in Northern Ireland. The first Chief Commissioner for Human Rights was Professor Brice Dickson. In 2005, he was succeeded by Professor Monica McWilliams, formerly one of the founding members and leaders of the Northern Ireland Women's Coalition. There are nine other Human Rights Commissioners in Northern Ireland (NIHRC, 2008).

The Equality Commission

Another support mechanism to bolster devolution in NI is the **Equality Commission.** Ending political and socio-economic inequality in NI had been the driving force behind the Civil Rights movement of the late 1960s, and the need for formal protection of equality had been recognised with the establishment of the Fair Employment Commission, Equal Opportunities Commission, and the Commission for Racial Equality and the Disability Council. The GFA replaced these Commissions with a new single body: **the Equality Commission**. The remit of the Commission was to advise on, validate and monitor statutory obligations and investigate complaints of default. The Equality Commission is chaired by a chief commissioner, a deputy commissioner, and 14 part time commissioners (Equality Commission, 2008).

Victims' Commission

An important element of devolution was the establishment of a Victims' Commission. Progress on this was slow. In 2005, the Secretary of State's appointment of an interim commissioner attracted controversy and criticism. When devolved power was restored in 2007, efforts were made to appoint a new commissioner. In January 2008, four commissioners instead of the one commissioner originally envisaged, were appointed. The FM and DFM were involved in their appointment and denied claims that the appointment of four commissioners was due to their inability to agree. Whatever the reason, the appointment of four commissioners, at a salary of £65,000 per annum for each commissioner, represented a significant financial and moral investment in efforts to support victims of the conflict in Northern Ireland (bbc.co.uk, 25 June 2008)

Consultative Group on the Past

In another important development a Consultative Group on the Past was set up by the British government. The group, chaired by Robin Eames and Denis Bradley, was appointed to find an agreed way to help the North overcome the legacy of 30 years of violence (*Belfast Telegraph*, 24 August 2007). The body engaged in consultation across Northern Ireland, met with 100 different groups and received 200 written submissions and 90 letters (*Belfast Telegraph*, 25 January 2008).

Policing and Justice

The GFA also laid out arrangements relating to the transfer of policing and justice matters in Northern Ireland (GFA, 1998: p22). Progress was made in relation to these, with the reform of the RUC and Sinn Féin's support for policing and justice arrangements in 2007, that made restoration of devolved government. The participation of Sinn Féin members in Policing Boards was a further indicator of its willingness to support this. The final stage in this process was the devolution of responsibility for policing and justice (GFA, 1998: p23) which had remained a 'reserved matter' under devolved arrangements.

This was the juncture at which Northern Ireland found itself by Spring 2008. In line with the timetable set by the St Andrews Agreement for transfer by May 2008, the 'reserved powers' relating to policing and justice would be transferred, marking the second stage of devolution and a further mark of the reduction of the British government's involvement in Northern Ireland. The symbolism attached to this is great. The British government has been involved in policing and justice in Northern Ireland from 1969 when British troops were deployed to shore up the RUC. Taking responsibility for policing and justice would be another measure of just how far away Northern Ireland had moved from the conflict of the past.

Summary

In its first phase devolved government was undermined by the protracted process of decommissioning of military weapons and the continued, though increasingly sporadic paramilitary activity. Against this backdrop, the Assembly and Executive operated – administering Northern Ireland through a democratically elected legislative chamber in which the major political parties in Northern Ireland were represented and from which the government, the Executive Committee, was formed. Ultimately, the challenges presented by the stop-start nature of decommissioning caused the Assembly and Executive to founder, leading to extended suspension from 2002–2007.

When it was restored, safeguards had been put in place (through the St Andrews Agreement) and commitment to democratic principles and support for policing and justice had been secured. The new Assembly and Executive were able to resume government of Northern Ireland, channelled through Ministers and their departments and through bodies such as the NSMC and the BIC. A further tier of public bodies, encompassing the Human Rights Commission and the Equality Commission, helped to underpin democracy and democratic procedures in NI.

The strength of the revised and restored institutions and a shared willingness to support devolved government enabled the Assembly and Executive to withstand crises in the months following re-devolution in 2007. Though political differences remain and are vocally expressed, nevertheless, the political stability that has emerged has allowed many to be more cautiously optimistic about the future of devolved government in Northern Ireland than has been the case for several years.

Chapter 7
Conclusion

As Ian Paisley bowed out of political life in Northern Ireland in June 2008, it was an opportunity for looking back as much as looking forward. In paying tribute to the former First Minister and with an eye to the future, Martin McGuinness (Deputy First Minister), in his nomination speech to the Assembly[1], made reference to speech that Dr Paisley had made in 2006 when he outlined his hopes that "the sons and daughters of the Planter and Gael have found a way to share the land of their birth and live together in peace." (OFMDFM, 5 June 2008)

His aspirations encapsulated the story of Northern Ireland, acknowledging the role and the roots of the past in the different histories of the Gael – the native Irish, and the Planter – the Protestant settlers; recognising the common past of their descendants and a wish to live together peacefully.

In the ten years since the Good Friday Agreement, much has been achieved in Northern Ireland to acknowledge the role of the past. While it may not have been possible to right historical wrongs, there has emerged a common will to move on and move together to govern Northern Ireland and secure for its people a society free from conflict.

Much has been achieved in relation to this that the day to day minutiae of political life can be overlooked. The political structures and systems that were set up through the Good Friday Agreement to facilitate and support devolution have proved generally robust, bolstered in 2006 by the St Andrews Agreement. Northern Ireland's political parties have adapted to a new way of politics in Northern Ireland, now more directly accountable to the electorate and to their constituents. The 'peace process' has necessitated ideological shifts in relation to power-sharing and while the bipolar blocs of unionism and nationalism remain, the political landscape is opening up to new parties such as the Green Party.

The wider context in which Northern Ireland exists has been and will continue to be an important factor in its future. Devolution as a model of sharing power in the UK is working effectively in the Scottish and Welsh Assemblies and NI's politicians benefi from collaboration through official institutions – such as the British Irish Council or bilaterally – as seen in an emerging relationship with the Scottish Government. Politically and economically, NI is not unaffected by the forces of globalisation.

Much has been achieved but there is still much to be done. If the first year of the restored devolved government (2007-2008) was a time for reassurance, NI's leaders were increasingly aware that it was also time to deliver: on economic development and investment; on reform of the health and education systems; in public policies relating to transport, housing, and social development. Solutions also need to be found for unresolved issues relating to policing and justice.

In accepting his nomination as First Minister of NI to succeed Ian Paisley, Peter Robinson shared his vision for Northern Ireland:

"I want to see a Northern Ireland that is not known throughout the world for 'The Troubles' nor even for the peace process. I want to see a Northern Ireland that is known for innovation, for its industry, for the economic opportunities it offers, for the friendliness, warmth and charm of its people and the beauty, vitality and magic of its landscape (OFMDFM, 5 June 2008).

It is a vision and hope shared by many in Northern Ireland and promises a future very different from the violence and conflict of the past. The political infrastructure (the Assembly and Executive) is in place to make this happen but realising this vision will require NI's politicians to work together in building that "shared and better future" (Wilford and Wilson, May 2008: 18) to which Northern Ireland's politicians have committed themselves.

Notes

[1] Under the terms of the GFA, the positions of First Minister and Deputy First Minister are jointly elected so that if one resigns, the other must be renominated to the post (GFA, Strand 1, Article 15).

Appendix 1

ALLOCATION OF SEATS IN THE ASSEMBLY EXECUTIVE AND CHAIRS AND DEPUTY CHAIRS OF COMMITTEES

D'HONDT SYSTEM

Seats in the Assembly Executive and Chairs and Deputy Chairs of the Departmental Committees are allocated on the basis of the D'Hondt system.

The principle of the system is that seats are won singly and successively on the basis of the highest average. The method requires that the number of seats each party gained in the Assembly will be divided initially by one and thereafter by one more than the number of seats won, until all the seats are won.

Example (based on results of elections to NI Assembly March 2007

	Seats in Assembly	Divisor	Average
Party A	36	1	36*
Party B	28	1	28
Party C	18	1	18

*Party A wins the first seat and its divisor becomes 2

	Seats in Assembly	Divisor	Average
Party A	36	2	18
Party B	28	1	28*
Party C	18	1	18

*Party B wins the second seat and its divisor becomes 2

	Seats in Assembly	Divisor	Average
Party A	36	2	18
Party B	28	2	14
Party C	18	1	18*

*Party C wins the third seat and its divisor becomes 2

	Seats in Assembly	Divisor	Average
Party A	36	2	18*
Party B	28	2	14
Party C	18	2	9

*Party A wins the fourth seat and its divisor becomes 3

(adapted from http://www.niassembly.gov.uk/io/summary/d'hondt.htm accessed 11th July 200

Appendix 2

EXAMINATION GUIDE

The examination board for NI, CCEA, offers the module 'The Government and Politics of Northern Ireland' for examination at Advanced Subsidiary (AS) level.

The examination lasts one hour and fifteen minutes.

Students are asked to answer three questions. Questions 1 and 2 must be answered. For Question 3, students can choose to answer either 3A or 3B. A total of 50 marks is allocated for the paper.

Questions 1 and 2 are based on sources and students are expected to refer to the sources in their answers. Sources may be of a variety of types including text, pictorial, graphical and statistical.

The examination is based on the learning outcomes for the course and students should be able to:

- demonstrate knowledge and understanding of the government of NI since 1994, including political arrangements such as direct rule and devolution of power to the Northern Ireland Assembly;
- demonstrate knowledge and understanding of a range of political concepts such as democracy, power, authority, democratic deficit and power-sharing and apply these in the political context of NI;
- demonstrate knowledge and understanding of the role of political parties and of the strategies and policies of the main NI political parties;
- analyse how the strategies and policies of the main NI political parties have changed since 1994;
- assess how and why electoral support for the main political parties has changed since 1994;
- assess the political impact of the different electoral systems in use in Northern Ireland.

EXAMINATION HINTS

- Allocate approximately 10 minutes to reading the source and questions before you begin writing your answers.
- Highlight or underline key words in the source or questions.
- If the question asks you to refer to the source, you must refer to it otherwise you will limit the possible number of marks you can attain.
- Note the author and date of the source since this will put the source in context.
- Note any bias or subjectivity in the source.

- Watch your time: allocate more time to the questions with the most marks (for example: Q1: 10 minutes; Q2: 20 minutes; Q3: 30 minutes.

- Allocate 2–3 minutes at the end of the examination to read over your answers. Check for spelling, grammar and general expression. Remember, you are also being examined on your quality of written communication.

Appendix 3

Sample examination paper (based on specimen paper)

Study the source below and answer the questions that follow.

Source

> *The Powers of the Northern Ireland Assembly*
>
> The First Minister and the Deputy First Minister, the Departments and the Departmental Committees are nominated by, answerable to, and can all be removed from office by the Assembly.
>
> Under devolution, the Assembly can make primary legislation in a number of important areas including finance, economic development, education, environment, health and social services. Furthermore, as the Assembly becomes established it may take responsibility for functions such as policing and security.
>
> Adapted from McMahon, M (2002) *Government and Politics of Northern Ireland* Colourpoint.

1. With reference to the Source and any other relevant material you have studied, explain two functions of the Northern Ireland Assembly. *(8 marks)*

2. With reference to the Source and any other relevant material you have studied, outline the changes in the DUP's policy on devolution since 1998. *(16 marks)*

3. ***Either***

   a) Assess the reasons for the changes in Sinn Féin's electoral performance since 1997. (26 marks)

   Or

   b) Compare the effects of the 'First Past the Post' and Single Transferable Vote electoral systems that are used in Northern Ireland. *(26 marks)*

References

ACE Encyclopaedia (2008) 'Electoral Knowledge Network', http://aceproject.org/ace-en/topics/es/esd/esd02/esd02d/esd02d01 [accessed 10 July 2008]

Access Research Knowledge (1998) 'The 1998 Referendums', http://www.ark.ac.uk/elections/fref98.htm [accessed 10 July 2008]

St Andrews Agreement (2006) *The St Andrews Agreement, Practical Changes to the operation of the institutions*, http://www.standrewsagreement.org/annex_a.htm [accessed 10 July 2008]

Belfast Telegraph, 5 November 2001

Belfast Telegraph (2007) 'Visiting Scottish leader calls for closer links with Ulster'. 19 June 2007 http://www.belfasttelegraph.co.uk/news/politics/article2676365.ece [accessed 10 July 2008]

Belfast Telegraph (2007) 'Troubles panel begins seeking suggestions from the public'. 24 August 2007, http://www.belfasttelegraph.co.uk/breaking-news/ireland/article2891937.ece [accessed 10 July 2008]

Belfast Telegraph (2008) 'Troubles body concludes public consultation', 25 January 2008 http://www.belfasttelegraph.co.uk/breakingnews/ireland/article3372111.ece [accessed 10 July 2008]

Belfast Telegraph (2008) 'Victims' commissioners 'may have to get tough', 28 January 2008 http://www.belfasttelegraph.co.uk/news/local-national/article3379550.ece [accessed 10 July 2008]

Belfast Telegraph (2008) 'The work starts now, says new Victims' Commission' 29 January 2008 http://www.belfasttelegraph.co.uk/news/local-national/article3382250.ece [accessed 10 July 2008]

Belfast Telegraph (2008) 'Will row over 'nepotism' in London affect Ulster MLAs' 1 February 2008, http://www.belfasttelegraph.co.uk/news/opinion/article3393396.ece [accessed 10 July 2008]

Belfast Telegraph (2008), 'Proposal to increase MLAs' salaries' 8 February 2008 http://www.belfasttelegraph.co.uk/news/politics/article3413870.ece [accessed 10 July 2008]

Belfast Telegraph (2008) 'Donaldson replaces Paisley Jnr as Junior Minister'. 26 February 2008, http://www.belfasttelegraph.co.uk/breakingnews/ireland/politics/article3466668.ece [accessed 10 July 2008]

BBC (1999) 'The D'Hondt System Explained', http://news.bbc.co.uk/1/hi/northern_ireland/91150.stm [accessed 15 August 2008]

BBC (2000) *Hearts and Minds,* October 2000

BBC (2000) Civic Forum http://www.bbc.co.uk/northernireland/schools/agreement/governance/civic2.shtml [accessed 10 July 2008]

BBC (2003) 'The Democratic Deficit', 3 May 2003 http://news.bbc.co.uk/1/hi/northern_ireland/2998469.stm [accessed 10 July 2008]

BBC (2004) 'European Election: Northern Ireland Result', 14 June 2004 http://news.bbc.co.uk/1/hi/northern_ireland/3766315.stm [accessed 10 July 2008]

BBC (2005) 'McWilliams named Human Rights Chief' 16 June 2005 http://news.bbc.co.uk/1/hi/northern_ireland/4098584.stm [accessed 10 August 2008]

BBC (2006) 'Gender Agenda: Ten Years of the Women's Coalition', 23 February 2006 http://news.bbc.co.uk/1/hi/programmes/politics_show/4742540.stm [accessed 15 August 2008]

BBC (2006) 'Bell named new Assembly Speaker', 10 April 2006 http://news.bbc.co.uk/1/hi/northern_ireland/4896488.stm [accessed 10 July 2008]

BBC (2007) Northern Ireland Election Overview, 13 March 2007 http://news.bbc.co.uk/1/shared/vote2007/nielection/html/main.stm [accessed 10 July 2008]

BBC (2007) 'A tale of two polls', 9 March 2007 http://news.bbc.co.uk/1/hi/northern_ireland/6435373.stm [accessed 10 July 2008]

BBC (2007) 'Lo takes seat for South Belfast', 9 March 2007 http://news.bbc.co.uk/1/hi/northern_ireland/6431557.stm [accessed 10 July 2008]

BBC (2007) 'Picking Portfolios: How it Works', 13 March 2007

http://news.bbc.co.uk/1/hi/northern_ireland/6389409.stm [accessed 10 July 2008]

BBC (2007) 'Sinn Féin votes to support the policy', 28 January 2007 http://news.bbc.co.uk/1/hi/northern_ireland/6308175.stm [accessed 10 July 2008]

BBC (2007) 'SDLP warned over Fianna Fáil link', 29 November 2007 http://news.bbc.co.uk/1/hi/northern_ireland/7118163.stm [accessed 10 July 2008]

BBC (2007) 'Salmond calls for closer NI ties', 18 June 2007 http://news.bbc.co.uk/1/hi/northern_ireland/6761769.stm [accessed 10 July 2008]

BBC (2008) 'Committee in stormy 11 plus talks' http://news.bbc.co.uk/1/hi/northern_ireland/7219981.stm [accessed 10 July 2008]

BBC (2008) 'Ruane outlines transfer test plan', 16 May 2008 http://news.bbc.co.uk/1/hi/northern_ireland/7404108.stm [accessed 15 August 2008]

BBC (2008) 'Enlarging Europe'. http://news.bbc.co.uk/1/shared/spl/hi/europe/04/enlarging_europe/html/eu_expansion.stm [accessed 10 July 2008]

BBC (2008) *Q&A: Enlarging Europe, 1 January 2008* http://news.bbc.co.uk/1/hi/world/europe/2266385.stm [accessed 10 July 2008]

BBC (2008) 'Paisley Jnr admits he made a mistake', 16 January 2008 http://news.bbc.co.uk/1/hi/northern_ireland/7191070.stm [accessed 10 July 2008]

Bell, K, Jarman, N, & Lefebvre, T, (2004) *Migrant Workers in Northern Ireland, Belfast Institute for Conflict Research*, pp1–129. http://www.ofmdfmni.gov.uk/migrantworkers.pdf [accessed 10 July 2008]

Buckland, P, (1981) *A History of Northern Ireland*. Dublin: Gill and McMillan

British Irish Council (2008) Webpage. http://www1.british-irishcouncil.org/ [accessed 9 June 2008]

Centre for the Advancement of Women in Politics (2008) Elections http://www.qub.ac.uk/cawp/election.html [accessed 10 July 2008]

Davenport, M, (2003) 'The Democratic Deficit', 3 May 2003 http://news.bbc.co.uk/1/hi/northern_ireland/2998469.stm [accessed 10 July 2008]

Department of Education Northern Ireland (2008) Post Primary Transfer, http://www.deni.gov.uk/index/22-postprimaryarrangements-new-arrangements_pg/post_primary_arrangements-whats_new.htm [accessed 10 July 2008]

Department of Foreign Affairs (1993) Downing Street Declaration http://foreignaffairs.gov.ie/home/index.aspx?id=8734 [accessed 10 July 2008]

Department of Foreign Affairs (1996) The Mitchell Report http://www.dfa.ie/home/index.aspx?id=347 [accessed 10 July 2008]

Department of Foreign Affairs (1998) the Good Friday Agreement http://www.dfa.ie/home/index.aspx?id=335 [accessed 10 July 2008]

Electoral Office of Northern Ireland (2008) Published electorate, 1 February 2008 http://www.eoni.org.uk/february_2008_electorate_by_ward.pdf [accessed 10 July 2008]

Electoral Commission (2006) http//www.electoralcommission.org.uk/home [accessed 15 August 2008]

Equality Commission for Northern Ireland (2008) http://www.equalityni.org/sections/default.asp?secid=0 [accessed 10 July 2008]

European Union (2008) Enlargement 2004 and 2007 http://europa.eu/scadplus/leg/en/s40016.htm [accessed 10 July 2008]

European Union (2008) Europa Glossary, http://europa.eu/scadplus/glossary/democratic_deficit_en.htm [accessed 10 July 2008]

Green Party of Northern Ireland (2007) *Manifesto* http://www.greens-in.org/tiki-page.php?pageName=Manifesto+Download [accessed 10 July 2008]

Guardian Unlimited (2003) 'Blair seeks way to reveal details of IRA weapons' 23 October 2003

http://www.guardian.co.uk/politics/2003/oct/23/northernireland.northernireland2

[accessed 10 July 2008]

Guardian, 23 October 2003

Guardian, 24 November 2003

Guardian Unlimited (2008) 'In praise of ... the Good Friday Agreement.' The Guardian Online, 11 April 2008, http://www.guardian.co.uk/commentisfree/2008/apr/11/northernireland.northernireland [accessed 10 July 2008]

Hague, R, Harrop, M, & Breslin, S, (1998) *Comparative Government and Politics.* New York: Macmillan

Hennessy, T, (2000) *The Northern Ireland Peace Process,* Gill and MacMillan

Heywood, A., (2000) *Key Concepts in British Politics,* Palgrave MacMillan

HMSO (2008) Acts of the Northern Ireland Assembly, http://www.hmso.gov.uk/legislation/northernireland/ni-acts.htm [accessed 10 July 2008]

Irish News, 20 November 2003

Irish Times, 27 October 2007

Mitchell, G, de Chastelain, J, & Holkeri, H, (1996) *Report of the International Body (The Mitchell Report),* http://www.dfa.ie/home/index.aspx?id=8741 [accessed 10 July 2008]

nations and Regions Dynamics of Devolution (August 2001) http://www.ucl.ac.uk/constitution-unit/monrep/ni/nimay01.pdf [accessed 15 August 2008]

Northern Ireland Assembly (2007) 'Committee for Education Welcomes Minister', 18 May 2007 http://www.niassembly.gov.uk/education/2007mandate/press/pn13_07.htm [accessed 10 July 2008]

Northern Ireland Assembly (2008) Education Service http://education.niassembly.gov.uk/ [accessed 10 July 2008]

NI Assembly Debates Monday 28 January 2008 http://www.theyworkforyou.com/ni/?id=2008-01-28.8.1&s=programme+for+government+speaker%3A13840#g8.60" [accessed 10 August 2008]

Northern Ireland Assembly (2008) Standing Orders of the Northern Ireland Assembly http://www.niassembly.gov.uk/sopdf/so.htm [accessed 10 July 2008]

Northern Ireland Assembly (2007) *Committee on Procedures to Launch Inquiries into Electronic Voting and Committee Systems and Structures,* 27 June 2007 http://www.niassembly.gov.uk/procedures/2007mandate/press/proc_2_07.htm [accessed 10 July 2008]

Northern Ireland Assembly Debates Monday 28 January 2008 http://www.theyworkforyou.com/ni/id=2008-01-28.8.1&s=programme+for+governement+speaker%3A13840#g8.60 [accessed 10 August 2008]

Northern Ireland Assembly (2008) Transitional Assembly http://www.niassembly.gov.uk/transitional/info_office/commentary.htm [accessed 10 July 2008]

Northern Ireland Executive (2008) 'North-South Ministerial Council', http://www.northsouthministerialcouncil.org/index.htm [accessed 10 July 2008]

Northern Ireland Executive (2008) 'Scotland and NI link together', 20 February 2008 http://www.northernireland.gov.uk/news/news-ofmdfm/news-ofmdfm-200208-scotland-and-northern.htm [accessed 10 July 2008]

Northern Ireland Human Rights Commission (NIHRC) (2008) Northern Ireland Human Rights Commission, Protecting and promoting your rights, http://www.nihrc.org/index.php?option=com_content&task=view&id=20&Itemid=25 [accessed 10 July 2008]

Northern Ireland Office (2007) Joint Communiqué British-Irish Intergovernmental Conference – Dundalk, 26 February 2007 http://www.nio.gov.uk/media-detail.htm?newsID=14166 [accessed 10 July 2008]

Northern Ireland Office (2008) Northern Ireland Office, http://www.nio.gov.uk/index.htm

Northern Ireland Police Board (2006–2007) *Quality of Service Report* http://www.nipolicingboard.org.uk/index/publications/annual-reports.htm [accessed 10 July 2008]

Northern Ireland Statistical and Research Agency (2008) Non-UK nationals allocated NINo by nationality, www.nisra.gov.uk [accessed 10 July 2008]

OFCOM (2001) The Communications Market: Nations and Regions Northern Ireland, http://www.ofcom.org.uk/research/cm/nations/northern_ireland/northern_ireland.pdf [accessed 10 July 2008]

Office of the First Minister and Deputy First Minister (OFMDFM) (2008) Speeches delivered by the First Minister and Deputy First Minister 5 June 2008, http://www.northernireland.gov.uk/news/news-ofmdfm/news-ofmdfm-050608-speeches-delivered-by.htm [accessed 10 July 2008]

PUP web site: www.pup-ni.org.uk/home/default.aspx [accessed 15 August 2008]

Republic of Ireland (2004) Constitution of Ireland, http://www.taoiseach.gov.ie/attached_files/Pdf%20files/Constitution%20of%20IrelandNov2004.pdf [accessed 10 July 2008]

RTE News (2007) 'Belfast-Dublin train may run hourly', 14 SEptember 2007 http://www.rte.ie/news/2007/0914/trains.html [accessed 10 July 2007]

Sinn Féin (1994) Towards a lasting peace in Ireland, http://www.sinnfein.ie/pdf/ TowardsLastingPeace.pdf [accessed 10 July 2008]

Social Democratic and Labour Party (1998) *Party Manifesto*

Leverhulme Funded Monitoring Programme (1999) *Northern Ireland Report (1)*

http://www.ucl.ac.uk/constitution-unit/monrep/ni/ninov99.pdf [accessed 10 July 2008]

Leverhulme Funded Monitoring Programme (2000) *Northern Ireland Report (2)*

http://www.ucl.ac.uk/constitution-unit/monrep/ni/nifeb00.pdf [accessed 10 July 2008]

Leverhulme Funded Monitoring Programme (2000) *Northern Ireland Report (4)*

http://www.ucl.ac.uk/constitution-unit/monrep/ni/niaug00.pdf [accessed 10 July 2008]

Wilson, R, (2001) *Agreeing to Disagree: A Guide to the Northern Ireland Assembly,* The Stationery Office

Wilson, R, *et al* (2001, May) *Nations and Regions: The Dynamics of Devolution - Northern Ireland*

http://www.ucl.ac.uk/constitution-unit/monrep/ni/nimay01.pdf [accessed 10 July 2008]

Wilson, R, *et al* (2001, August) *Nations and Regions: The Dynamics of Devolution - Northern Ireland*

https://ucl.ac.uk/constitution-unit/monrep/ni/niaug01.pdf [accessed 10 July 2008]

Wilson, R, *et al* (2001, November) *Nations and Regions: The Dynamics of Devolution - Northern Ireland*

http://www.ucl.ac.uk/constitution-unit/monrep/ni/ninov01.pdf [accessed 10 July 2008]

Wilson, R, *et al* (2003, February) *Nations and Regions: The Dynamics of Devolution - Northern Ireland*

http://www.ucl.ac.uk/constitution-unit/monrep/ni/ni_february_2003.pdf [accessed 10 July 2008]

Wilson, R, *et al* (2003, August) *Nations and Regions: The Dynamics of Devolution - Northern Ireland*

http://www.ucl.ac.uk/constitution-unit/monrep/ni/ni_august_2003.pdf [accessed 10 July 2008]

Wilford, R, Wilson, R and Claussen, K, (2007) Power to the People – a democratic audit of Northern Ireland. TASC: Democratic Audit

Wilford, R, & MacGinty, R, (2004, February) *Devolution Briefing*, http://www. devolution.ac.uk/pdfdata/wilford_macginty_briefing_PDF.pdf

Wilford, R, & Wilson, R, *A Democratic Design? The Political Style of the NI Assembly* Democratic Dialogue May 2001 http://cain.ulst.ac.uk/dd/papers/audit.htm [accessed 12 August 2008]

Wilford, R, & Wilson, R, (2005, April) *Nations and Regions: The Dynamics of Devolution - Northern Ireland* p4ff

http://www.ucl.ac.uk/constitution-unit/monrep/ni/ni_april_2005.pdf [accessed 10 July 2008]

Wilford, R, & Wilson, R, (2007, January) *Devolution Monitoring Programme – Northern Ireland,* Devolution Monitoring Report p4ff

http://www.ucl.ac.uk/constitution-unit/research/devolution/MonReps/NI_Jan07.pdf [accessed 10 July 2008]

Wilford, R, & Wilson, R, (2007, April) *Devolution Monitoring Programme - Northern Ireland,* Devolution Monitoring Report

http://www.ucl.ac.uk/constitution-unit/research/devolution/MonReps/NI_April07.pdf [accessed 10 July 2008]

Wilford, R, & Wilson, R, (2008, January) *Devolution Monitoring Programme – Northern Ireland,* Devolution Monitoring Report

http://www.ucl.ac.uk/constitution-unit/research/devolution/devo-monitoring-programme.html [accessed 10 July 2008]

Index